This Grief Is Mine

A Personal Journey and Guide through the Aspects of Grief, Comfort and Healing

Norma C. Atherton

Fairway Press, Lima, Ohio

THIS GRIEF IS MINE

FIRST EDITION
Copyright © 2001 by
Norma L. Atherton

ISBN 0-7880-1675-X

Acknowledgments

In grateful appreciation for everyone who gave me comfort while I was grieving, support and encouragement while I was earning my long overdue Bachelor's degree, and praise and incitement while I was writing this book.

Special thanks go to Lois Lafreniere who painstakingly typed my first "pre-degree" manuscript; to Jean Gilman who was God's catalyst throughout my return to college and my writing; to Frank Trocco, Sheila Kunkle, and Alice Eichholz who were my mentors at Vermont College, not only helping me academically, but also helping me emerge from my grief with a new perspective, with renewed confidence, with my own voice, and with hope; to my children and grandchildren who gave me the time and space to study and to write; to my late husband, Glenn, whose lifetime of gifts keep giving even after his death; and to God who allowed my family, friends, and mentors to touch my life and make a difference.

Table Of Contents

Preface

Two years after my husband died, I returned to college at age fifty to earn the credits I was lacking for my degree. Although my decision to return to college did not seem to be a conscious one on my part, I was very sure about my purpose in returning to the academic world. I wanted to study poetry, to gain an appreciation for free verse (a well-known poet, though I have no idea whom, likened writing free verse to playing tennis without a net, and I admit I used to agree), and to learn to write poetry outside the realm of grief and comfort.

My first poem was written when I could find no other words that sounded appropriate for friends who had suddenly lost their oldest child at age nine. After staring down at a sympathy card to no avail for what seemed like hours and unable to write any kind of personal message, I finally prayed for help and inspiration. Immediately, I began writing words in the form of a poem as if Someone else was guiding my hand — as well as my mind.

After that first poem, there were many poems that would come to me in the quiet of the night, or at the kitchen sink (I do a lot of meditating in front of the dirty dishes!) if I was emotionally tied to the one who was grieving or the one who died. As time passed, words and phrases would swirl around in my head for mere acquaintances and would not stop until I wrote them down. The poems came from within, filled with emotion, faith, and hope, and touched the heartstrings of many grieving friends and family members as well as providing for my own comfort. They were, however, in no way literary masterpieces. Studying poetry on a collegiate level, I thought, would surely provide me with the tools I needed to create an academically acceptable poem of a higher caliber. I found the label of "greeting card poetry" attached to my writings offensive and I wanted to explore the difference between popular poetry and poetry of literary distinction.

Well, at least that was my plan. However, apparently it was not the master plan for me as I somehow ended up studying religion instead of poetry. Each semester I would put off my poetry study to do one more semester of religion until my final semester, and even then, Poetry was no where on my schedule. My last semester combined my life, my numerous losses, my religious studies, and my beliefs as I did an in-depth study on grief and grief therapy through writing.

So, here I am, with my degree in my hand (actually it is on the wall), still unable to discuss poetry on any kind of academic level. Nevertheless, I *can* discuss the power of poetry in the healing process of grief, and I guess that is what the Master Planner had in mind for me all along. And I learned a valuable lesson. I do not write poems to achieve literary distinction. I write poems to provide comfort and meaning in the wake of despair from losing a loved one. It is the rhythm of the poems as much as the meaning of the words that soothes the broken heart. I could have no greater value in my writing than to have touched someone's heart, to give someone a written reminder that life and love do not end in death.

This book is a combination of my own grief, my academic study of grief, some of my poems of both anguish and comfort, and my faith. Its purpose is to bring comfort and understanding to those who are grieving or who have loved ones who are grieving. Sometimes we need to know that we are not the only ones who have gone through pain and sorrow, and we definitely need to know that it is not only possible to survive, but to find meaning for our lives and for the lives and deaths of our departed loved ones. If anything in the written discussions or in the poetry reaches out to touch just one reader to bring some measure of comfort, understanding or hope, then this book will have fulfilled its purpose.

> *"Blessed are those who mourn, for they shall be comforted."*   Matthew 5:4

My thoughts and prayers are with everyone who grieves the loss of a loved one. May you find the comfort and peace that I have found through my friends, my family, my faith, and my writings. They are all a part of who I am as well as an important part of the completion of this book.

Chapter One

The Nature Of Grief

There is nothing that affects us as much as the death of a loved one. We mourn the loss of the physical presence, grieve for the heightened reality of our own mortality, fear for the unknown, cope with the changes death forces on our lives, and struggle to find meaning in death as well as in life. And, like it or not, we are plummeted into a state of deep sorrow filled with a menagerie of emotions and reactions we call grief

There are many books written about grief, dissecting it into stages, unraveling its emotions, and projecting recommendations for healing. Depending on which professional therapist one chooses to read, the stages may range from four to ten, but the vast realm of emotions is included somewhere in one stage or another no matter how the stages are labeled or how many stages are advocated.

When I recently did a six-month study on grief at a local college which included grief therapy through the creative mode of writing, I decided to create my own stages, numbering seven. I claimed no expertise other than personal experience (which amounts to quite a lot), and bravely set out to explain my choices. The most widely accepted stages of grief are the five stages presented by Elisabeth Kübler-Ross and include in order, denial, anger, depression, bargaining, and acceptance. Using these stages as a base, I added a first stage of shock and a final stage of transcendence. Relating information derived from *Good Grief* by Granger Westberg, *The Mourning Handbook* by Helen Fitzgerald, *Letting Go with Love* by Nancy O'Connor, *Transcending Loss* by Ashley Davis Prend, and *Understanding Grief* by Edgar Jackson, as well as a few others, to my own personal experiences, I was sure I had the perfect breakdown of the stages of grief for my final presentation.

In reality, however, there is nothing perfect about grief or its stages. Defining stages that shift from day to day is virtually impossible as emotions intermingle and constantly change direction. For instance, if one includes guilt in the stage of anger, and loneliness in the stage of depression, then these feelings overlap into the other stages throughout the grief process. If the feelings and emotions attributed to certain stages are not constant, then stages cannot be clearly defined.

Therefore, I like to think of grief as being made up of two *aspects* rather than a certain number of stages. There is a *universal* aspect which contains all the feelings and emotions that everyone experiences in whatever order they may come, and the *individual* aspect which exists because we are all unique individuals and no two persons grieve in exactly the same way.

The individual aspect of grief often gets the least attention, yet it is important to understand, both for the one who is grieving and for his or her friends and family. There is no "proper" way to grieve. We are all individuals and we grieve differently, the way we *need* to. Whether a person is crying, screaming, silent, or even laughing, these expressions are a part of the coping mechanisms of the individual. Nancy O'Connor, Ph.D., explains the different reactions to death in her book *Letting Go with Love* by saying,

> *Each person is an accumulation of genetic material, culture, family backgrounds, personal experiences, and unique coping styles. So when we experience the death of a loved and treasured person, we react in slightly different ways based on these factors.*

When my husband died suddenly, my son who lives in South Carolina (we live in Vermont) had not seen him for almost a year. We were scheduled to leave six days after the day he died to visit our son and his new baby girl. When my son and his family arrived for the funeral, part of his anguish was due to the length of time it had been since he had seen his father, adding to the despair of knowing he would never see him again. So, to help bridge the gap between these two realities and his emotions, we watched videos showing his father as alive and well, and as usual, a source of enjoyment and laughter. So, we laughed. One of my son's friends recently described my husband as someone who, no matter how you felt before, always made you feel better just to be in his company. The videos had the same effect. The laughter was as strong an emotional release as tears, but I often wonder what outsiders would have thought to see the whole family laughing together at such a sad time in all our lives. I am sure there would have been many who would have thought we were heartless or lacking real love for a man, who in truth, was loved more deeply and mourned more intensely than anyone could ever know. People who did not know him enough to realize you could not think of him without smiling would never understand that the more we smiled, the more our hearts were full of him.

The same is true for the length of time grief lasts as it is for how a person grieves. It is never exactly the same. Experts in the field of grief therapy seem to disagree on whether grief really *ever* ends at all. Dr. O'Connor divides the time period for grief into four stages which are completed within two years, whereas Ashley Davis Prend, a licensed psychotherapist, says, "Grieving is not a short term process; it's not even a long term process; it's a *lifelong* process." Helen Fitzgerald, a certified death educator, leaves the door open as to the duration of grief by saying, "It will take as long as it needs to take." She also supports Prend's lifelong theory as she further states, "I don't think one ever 'gets over' grief; it just becomes part of your life, as all experiences do."

In so far as the loved one who died is a part of who we are and the memory of the reality of his or her life will always be a part of who we become, perhaps grief could be seen as a process that never ends, but is constantly reincorporated into new aspects of our lives. However, I feel that the most accurate answer is undoubtedly the one offered by Fitzgerald that leaves the door open to be short or long, to have an end or not. There is one thing I do know: two years is a very unrealistic amount of time for grief to be resolved, especially if the death is sudden, if it is the death of a child or spouse, or if the death involves violence such as murder or suicide.

For myself, my grief over my husband's death was complicated by two other surrounding losses, the death of my cherished mother the year prior to his death and the mysterious disappearance of our beloved family dog the following year. To add to my losses, dealing with an impersonal corporation controlling my husband's trust fund was an ongoing nightmare, keeping his absence in the forefront of my life in a major role. Perhaps my grief will find an end some day, but for now, it is still a part of who I am and is still shaping who I will become.

I cannot stress the individual nature of grief enough. I think we all have our own perception of how we think someone should grieve. When we see someone grieving in a way that does not fall into that perception, we are very quick to offer advice or simply to place judgment. Although I was always very compassionate when a friend or family member had a loved one die, doing what I could to help, writing personal poems of comfort, and attending the funeral rituals, I was always ready to judge their reactions of grief. Too many tears were seen as self-pity and self-indulgence. Not enough tears varied from strength to lack of feeling. Sleeping with a loved one's pillow was morbid, dwelling on the death or putting the deceased on a pedestal was unfair to the living loved ones sending them a message that the one who died was more important, and stretching their grief out too long was unhealthy. I had no idea in the world what devastating emotions ruled the mind, hidden or revealed, or just how long it takes to heal those deep wounds.

Telling someone not to cry is counter-productive. Tears are cleansing and healing. They release emotions that if buried will cause emotional and physical distress later on. Laughter is also healing as is any display of emotion during the grief process. If we transfer our feelings of uncomfortableness at seeing tears to the person releasing those tears, we are doing more harm than good. If crying is what is needed, let the tears flow. If you truly want to comfort someone, let them grieve in his or her own way. Provide a comfort zone where your friend or family member will be able to express emotions freely, whether it is tears, laughter, pounding fists on tables, silence, screaming, or any other method.

Another area of concern for friends and family members which adds to their being uncomfortable around someone who is grieving is simply that they do not know what to say. What can you say? Most of us who are grieving do not know what we want to hear. You could say something one day that would be offensive that the very next day might be comforting. It depends on our momentary emotional state how we react to certain comments.

I remember all the expressions that sent me into a rage after my husband died. "How are you doing?" A perfectly honest question of concern left me with an urge to scream, "How to hell do you think I am doing?" And knowing full well that nobody *really* wanted to listen to how I was doing, my standard answer was "okay." Okay! What does that mean? How could I be doing okay when my world had just fallen apart? My losses were innumerable. I lost my best friend, my confidant, my lover, my financial security, the father of my children, my social life, my contact with my husband's business associates, fun-filled trips to business conventions, being part of a couple, my way of life, my identity. And I was okay? I hardly think so, but not one person ever said, "I know better. How are you really doing?"

The phrase that made me feel the worst, believe it or not, was, "You look good." I should have felt complimented, but I felt guilty as if they were saying with judgmental amazement that I should not look good if I was grieving, that I should not comb my hair or wear make-up. Again my screams were held within as I cried out silently, "I am not the one who died. I still wash my hair. How am I supposed to look?"

But the well-meaning words that hurt me the most were from the friends who told me as soon as my husband died that I should not worry, I was young and I would find another husband some day. I had just lost someone very special. It is true that some day I could replace the position of a husband, but I could never replace the person. I wanted him back, not a replacement. It was like saying his life had no meaning outside the role of a husband. I bit my tongue, so to speak, and excused myself as the tears flowed.

Today, I can honestly say I know my friends meant no harm and were only struggling to say something in an effort to comfort me. And I guess the point I am trying to make is that if you don't know what to say, then there is no need to say anything. A touch, a hug, or a squeeze of the hand says far more than any words which could be misconstrued by a person who is too emotionally upset to reason out their true intention — the desire to comfort.

Perhaps it is the volatile array of emotions experienced by those of us who are grieving that makes others feel awkward around us as they never know from one minute to another what emotion might surface. And no matter how "in control" a person is, grief finds its times to release our hold over our emotions. And, no matter how differently we as individuals express the emotions of grief, or in what order we experience them, the emotions felt are universal. They are evident in the grieving process of most everyone.

When I use the term *universal,* at least in connection with grief, I am referring to a Western cultural-inclusive reaction to death. In some cultures, death is not viewed as an end, but as a journey or continuation. Funeral rites become a rite of passage for the dead and a celebration for the living. For example, in Africa, Torajin funerals are always joyous occasions of drinking and dancing. Although Christians hold to the belief of an afterlife, the separation from the deceased person's physical presence seems to overshadow the belief that he or she is going on to a better life.

Some cultures, such as the Mbuti pygmies, simply erase the dead, never speaking of them again. There is no need to grieve for someone who is totally forgotten. We are conditioned by our cultural attitudes toward death as to how we react to it. So, as I discuss the universal aspect of grief, containing the feelings and emotions common to everyone who grieves, it suffices to say there are exceptions, especially outside our Western cultural boundaries.

Of the many feelings and emotions involved in grief that need to be experienced before healing can take place, one of the very first is *shock.* Ashley Davis Prend explains,

> *The first wave of shock occurs the moment you discover that your loved one is dead, or is going to die. A feeling of numbness sets in and you might feel as if you are in a dream. . . you may cry hysterically or you may be unable to shed a tear, you may make all of the funeral arrangements or be unable to function.*

In her description of shock, Prend reveals not only its universal aspect, but also describes the individual aspect by stating that we may have opposite reactions to the same emotion. From crying hysterically to not shedding a tear, we all have different coping mechanisms to help deal with pain. Shock itself helps us deal with our pain slowly, allowing time to absorb the reality of the impending death or the actual death. The length of time we remain in shock is another individual aspect and depends on many factors such as the suddenness of the death, our relationship to the deceased, and the way the news was delivered.

When my husband died, my state of shock was prolonged by the way I was told of his death. After a frantic call from my son and a speeding trip to the hospital, I was in the waiting room. Too anxious to sit, I was pacing back and forth. When the doctor finally came in the room after what seemed like an eternity, he sat himself down in one of the empty chairs. Grilling me with questions which, to me, had no relevance unless my husband was still alive, I repeatedly asked if he would be all right to no avail. Eventually, when the doctor presumedly ran out of his meaningless questions, he answered mine by blurting out, "No, he is dead." There was no eye contact, no hand on my shoulder, no "I am sorry to have to tell you." There was just me standing and the doctor sitting. I may be small and perhaps my voice is too soft, but I am sure at that moment my screams could be heard all over the hospital and perhaps beyond. There were no immediate tears, just numbness. The world seemed to stand still, void of any movement.

I asked to see my husband, I *needed* to see him, to hold and kiss him one last time. Perhaps I just needed proof. I had rushed to the hospital many times with my son and once with my husband to find that things were not as bad as they seemed and on my way to the hospital I was convinced this would be one more of those times. But it was not.

The doctor's first response to my seeing my husband was a negative one but, with reluctance, he agreed. I wanted to go in alone, but by this time the whole family was there including my sister and my in-laws, who all insisted on going in with me, not wanting me to be alone and needing to say good-bye for themselves. Already in a state of shock, my trauma was increased by the events which unfolded in the emergency room. I reached the

17

door first, but as I opened the door, my father-in-law rushed past me and with tears and deep sobs, he fervently kissed, hugged and stroked his son, his best friend. I stood back and looked on as if I was watching a play. I could see my daughter on the opposite side of the table from her grandfather lovingly holding her father's hand, shedding no tears for the man she idolized. I seemed to be frozen to the floor, but finally I walked closer and, as if playing a part in the play that was before me, I placed a kiss on my husband's forehead and said one last "I love you." But it just did not seem real.

Nothing seemed real. It was not happening to me, it was happening to everyone else in the room. It was their loss, their grief, their story. I was just an observer. My state of shock allowed me to function mechanically, to help everyone else with their grief, and to perform the tasks of funeral and financial arrangements without falling apart.

Shock is responsible for many responses we often see as a contradiction to our perception of acceptable grief reactions. If someone who just lost a loved one does not shed tears at the funeral, we might question their true feelings for the deceased. On the other hand, we might say he or she has remarkable strength or great faith. The truth is, that person is probably still in a state of shock which provides a temporary anesthesia before other emotions surface and take over. While someone is in shock, the reality of the death has not yet been absorbed.

Shock is not the only buffer provided to ease the pain of grief. We also have the unique reaction of denial. It is easy to equate denial with a response to hearing the diagnosis for a terminal illness. Perhaps if we do not believe it to be true, it will somehow go away or be a mistake. It is more difficult to understand how you can deny death when the physical body lies dormant in front of you, but it can and does happen.

For me, denial came in the way I continued to live at first, keeping everything the same as if nothing happened. I tried to keep the house the same, taking care of the outside as my husband would have cared for it. I tried to keep family life the same as if there was not a big void when we were together. I tried to keep social contacts with the same couples with whom we had maintained an active friendship. And, I will say, in that last area, I have been very fortunate. Most books you read written for widows tell of the certainty that shared couple friends will soon drift away. Although the frequency of socialization and the activities of getting together have changed, every couple whom we were close to when my husband was alive has remained faithful and supportive. I firmly believe that when friends drift apart after the death of a spouse, it is largely due to the mind set of the remaining spouse. If you feel like a fifth wheel, then you will be one. If you truly enjoy being with couples for who they are as individuals, then they will enjoy being with you for who you are. If you look at them as a couple and feel left out because you are no longer part of a couple, then you will be left out.

I have not perfected this view by any means. I especially remember one Christmas when two couples were coming home from Florida for the holidays. They, along with two other couples who bear out the winter here in Vermont, were all going to get together for supper and called to see if I would join them. Well, it was Christmas time, a time for memories to forge into the forefront of life, and I just could not bring myself to go, even if they were going to my favorite restaurant. I could deal with one couple for sure, two couples most likely, but four couples and me? I could not deal with that. Which sort of proves my point. They would have been perfectly happy to have me there, would have been glad for the opportunity to see me during the busy holidays before returning to Florida, but I could not cope with the happiness of other couples when I was not one. I would have felt like a ninth wheel. I would have felt sorry for myself. Those were my feelings, not theirs.

At any rate, I finally realized that trying to keep everything around me the same was not going to bring my husband back. I deluded myself into believing that if everything was the same, I would wake up from this nightmare and find it was all a dream. But it was not a dream. I was wide awake and he was dead, at least physically dead. I will never believe that death is an end while I am alive. If I am ever proven wrong, it will be too late to matter!

My denial in connection with my mother was more prevalent before she died. When it was quite evident that my mother was in the first stages of Alzheimer's Disease, I could not accept the possibility. And why should I? The doctor who examined her said her condition was due to moving into an apartment after living in the same house for so many years; confusion was a frequent reaction of older people adjusting to new surroundings. Older people? What did this young "whipper snapper" of a doctor know about age? My mother was not old. She was barely seventy and longevity ran in her family.

As she never seemed to get adjusted to her new surroundings, I tried everything and every kind of specialist, from neurologists to psychologists. I even moved her closer to me so I could see her every day. Watching the dementia take over the person whom I loved and, more importantly, respected, was a nightmare. Nevertheless, for five years I denied that it was permanent. I just had to find the right doctor with the right diagnosis who would prescribe the right medicine. But it did not come. However, when the correct diagnosis finally came, it allowed me to stop denying what I already knew to be true but could not accept.

I have heard it said many times that people with Alzheimer's Disease do not suffer because they are not aware of anything anymore which leads to the classic excuse for not going to see an Alzheimer's patient. "I do not go to see him/her anymore because it hurts too much that he/she does not even know who I am." We tend to isolate the terminally ill, and especially those with dementia, partly, I suppose, because we feel helpless and uncomfortable, and partly because we feel they will not know or care whether we are there or not. Anyone who believes that Alzheimer's patients do not suffer, or that visiting them is a waste of time, has never spent much time with them.

My mother was aware for quite some time that she was different and she knew she was being treated differently by the people around her. She just did not comprehend why. Friends stopped coming to see her and she felt the same feeling of isolation as if she had leprosy in days of old. It seemed to add to her confusion, not being able to understand what was happening to her. Her confusion led to frustration which led to tears, something my mother rarely displayed before she became ill. Her faith was very strong and she never indulged in self-pitying tears. She had always embraced each day and its trials as a gift from God to be lived fully. Everyone loved her and she had many friends. She definitely knew the difference when they could no longer bring themselves to see that she still needed and responded to love and attention. No one is ever helpless when it comes to helping terminally ill patients, as everyone has love to give and even the dying — especially the dying — need to feel loved.

In addition to shock, denial, and the feeling of isolation, there are many emotions which are included in the universal aspect of grief. They include anger, rage, guilt, regret, fear, panic, resentment, depression, and loneliness. It was holding on to my anger and guilt that stretched out my healing process when my husband died. It seemed as if I was angry at the whole world. I had not experienced much anger during my mother's illness. I was neither angry at her nor did I blame her for her actions. I knew the disease was not her fault, I knew she had no control over her actions, and I knew her lack of awareness of who I was in her life was not a willful act of forgetting. If I was angry at all, it centered around envy: envy that my mother-in-law was so healthy and would play the larger role in my children's lives, envy that my friends still had a relationship of friendship with their mothers, and even envy that they did not have the responsibility of caring for a parent with Alzheimer's.

But when my husband died, anger surfaced as if it were an explosion. I was angry at my husband for leaving me and for not realizing his angina was more serious than he wanted to admit. I knew his angina was stronger and more frequent than usual, so I urged him to see his doctor before we left to go south. He finally agreed, went on a Thursday, told the doctor his increased angina was only coming with increased activity, which was not the whole truth, scheduled a stress test for Tuesday, but died on Saturday. How could he not have known? How could his doctor not have known? So, I became angry at the doctor even though I knew he was not working with all the facts.

I was angry at my husband's partner for getting the business all to himself. I was angry because I felt I did not get paid the true value of what my husband's stock was worth, even though I was the one who insisted I did not want to cause hard feelings or do anything that would tarnish my husband's hard work in building up the business by hiring an outside appraiser.

I was angry at the officers of the trust fund who controlled my husband's hard-earned money, sitting like gods in determining what the money could be used for and what it would not pay for with a seemingly great indifference to my needs. When my furnace had to be replaced, it was decided by the "gods" that the trust fund would only pay for half of the four thousand dollar unit. According to the trust document, the money is to be used to keep me in the lifestyle I am accustomed to. Well, I am definitely accustomed to heat! This is only one example of the many confrontations I had prior to moving the trust fund to another institution. When I was not angry at the discretionary board (the gods), I was angry at the lawyer for convincing my husband to put everything into a trust fund, angry that my husband left me with such a headache, and angry that he left me at all.

With all of this anger, the worst anger was aimed at myself. As anger and guilt go hand in hand, I blamed myself for my husband's death. According to O'Connor, guilt comes from something we did or said that we wish we had not done, or from something that we think that we should have said or done that we didn't do. In all the commotion of that first phone call from an hysterical son, me in the midst of giving a permanent to a client, and a complacent attitude that everything would be fine, I never thought to call my husband's heart specialist to meet us at the hospital. His first heart attack nine years earlier had been very mild, causing no damage. His system had built its own bypass made up of smaller vessels to carry the blood flow. Running to the hospital was commonplace due to an accident-prone son with every seemingly critical horror story turning out to be minor. I was sure this time would be the same. Why was I not more responsible? More concerned?

The attending physician had left me with a feeling of his incompetence after the way he broke the news of my husband's death. I even suspected, in my state of shock, that he did not try to save my husband in order to be able to use him for a donor, excluding his heart, of course. I was sure if I had called the heart specialist, my husband would still be alive. After all, everyone on *911* is always revived by some hero.

My guilt did not end with making the wrong choice by not thinking clearly enough to call a certain doctor. I felt guilty for the way I resented everyone's help; I felt guilty for the foolish little things I used to fuss about. I especially felt guilty about not making love the night before my husband died. He had been at the Mutuo, an Italian club, playing cards and drinking. He rarely drank to excess, but when he did I always seemed to punish him by withholding sex as if I was somehow really punishing my father for his drinking problem. I felt guilty for being grateful that we did not make love for fear he might have died lying next to me. I felt guilty because I took my husband, his love, and our life together for granted.

With guilt and anger comes depression. In her book, *Letting Go with Love,* Nancy O'Connor suggests that depression is sometimes defined as anger turned inward and includes the feelings of helplessness, hopelessness, powerlessness, sadness, disappointment and/or loneliness. However it is defined, it is a very difficult range of emotions to deal with, perhaps because we do not always realize we are depressed until we are far enough into recovery from our depression that we can look back and see where we have been. The emotions of depression are often so deep that we are not aware of the reality of our emotional state. At least that is the way it was for me. It was only when I re-read pieces of writing I wrote at my lowest ebb that I could see my depression more clearly.

When my mother finally died, I thought I would be glad, or at least relieved. Ever since I finally accepted that there would be no miracle, I prayed God would take her home. I felt she would be better off with God than living in a non-life of vegetation. Instead, I discovered that my loss was greater, compounded by the realization that I had lost three people instead of one. I lost my mother as I knew her, I lost the body that still looked like her, and I lost the new personality that had taken over her body, the one with whom I had formed a close emotional attachment by seeing to her needs. I had sung to her as I combed her hair each day, old familiar hymns

23

which she had dearly loved. I had bought her milkshakes, fed her, and brought my grandchildren to entertain her. The two younger ones loved to visit her with me, having no fears, just unconditional love.

I had been constantly running in and out of the nursing home ever since the dreadful decision was made that she needed more care than I had time to give. Then, suddenly, there was no need to go. I thought I could not wait to have more time, but instead I was lost. I felt as if I had lost part of my childhood, and as my mother's death put me in the position of the older generation, perhaps I had. I was sad, tired, and depressed. I even had physical symptoms of sore and aching muscles with little strength in my hands. My whole body felt heavy. Tests revealed no sign of any specific cause for my ailments.

I was just recovering from this feeling of helplessness when I was plunged into the devastating emotional trauma of my husband's death. I think my shock and anger delayed my depression, but on the first anniversary of his death, depression set in with a vengeance.

The physical symptoms of heaviness, weak and sore muscles returned and I was more exhausted than ever. I forced myself to work and smile, but all I wanted to do was sleep. I spent most of my time curled up with my faithful little dog by my side for company. I resented outside company which forced me to be sociable; it was too much of an effort. I left my answering machine on and just let the phone ring. I was afraid everyone would think I should be over my grief when I actually felt worse than before. Out of my despair, I wrote a poem of comfort which was set to music by a friend. Depression and despair have always been a catalyst for creativity. Many of the best loved hymns were written during or after a personal crisis. Not that my poem will ever be a best-loved hymn, but it was a desperate cry for meaning within the framework of my beliefs which became a testament to my faith.

My dog, Jennie, loved the attention and the time I now spent at home with her instead of running errands. If I did venture out, I would have attacks of panic after a while, forcing me to rush home in order to feel secure once again. There are some grief therapists such as Westberg and Fitzgerald who list panic as separate stage of grief, but to me it seems to be a part of the larger feeling of depression. It is, however, a real emotion involved in grieving. At any rate, this feeling of panic when I was away from the house kept me close at home and close to Jennie.

My husband and I had often joked about never getting a divorce because neither of us wanted to give up Jennie. With his death, I had her all to myself, and often openly expressed my pleasure of triumph as if I had captured a prize. "See, you left me," I would say, "and now Jennie belongs to me." But, as change is one thing I can count on in my life, having Jennie to myself did not last long. She disappeared mysteriously a few months after the first anniversary of my husband's death. I looked for her for weeks, knocking on doors, putting up posters, and placing ads in the newspapers. Half the town also drove around the back roads hoping to be the one to find her for me.

The pain was more than I could bear. Losing Jennie was the final straw. Although I cried harder and more often than I ever had before to release my emotions, I could not get through my grief. It was as if I had lost a part of my husband all over again. She was his hunting dog as well as our pet. She had understood my pain; she felt it too. Now I was completely alone, alone with my grief.

I sharpened my bargaining techniques, the ones that failed with my mother's illness, trying desperately to strike a deal with God. My pleas for a miracle for my mother in exchange for my eternal gratitude and servitude had been ignored, but I still tried again to entice God to bring back Jennie and, in return, I would be a better person and do all I could to help others. The deal changed as the days passed by from having Jennie return safely, thus renewing my faith, to finding her alive and well with another family who could keep her as long as I knew she was well, and finally to just finding her body just to have some closure, some peace, and my life back. I offered many sacrifices to complete my side of the bargain, but still there was no Jennie, no husband, no mother.

As the bargaining failed time after time, the questions came back to haunt me. Why not a mother who abandoned or abused her children? Why not a man who existed on the couch in front of the television instead of a man who loved and lived every moment of life? Why not a dog who was chained to a dog house, spoken to only at mealtime? Perhaps they were just fleeting questions, perhaps I was questioning my faith, but I know in my heart I was not suggesting some kind of trade-off. When I stopped asking, "Why my loved ones?" the answer came in the form of another question. "Why *not* my loved ones?" I had watched friends lose parents, partners, siblings, and children for years. Why should my family be immune to disease and death?

With that realization, I slowly made my way into accepting my losses. I think some people have the wrong impression of accepting the death of a loved one. It does not mean that every feeling and emotion is behind you or that the absence of your loved one is no longer important. I like Ashley Davis Prend's explanation of acceptance. "Acceptance does not mean that you *like* what happened, nor does it mean that you forget your loved one. It means that you understand the magnitude of what happened, knowing your life will never be the same, knowing that you must learn to live with the loss." I understood the magnitude, for sure, and certainly knew my life would not be the same. Learning to live with it, however, was not easy. For so long I tried to keep everything the same, pretending it was for the children. But everything was not the same and all our lives seemed to be unraveling. I kept returning to anger, as if I blamed all my children's and my own problems on my husband's death. "If you were alive," I would say, "this would not be happening." Perhaps that was true to some extent, but the point is, it was not his fault. Yes, we have been put in situations that would not have been part of our lives if he were still living, but the choices made were ours. Accepting this fact was very difficult for me. It was easier to blame a dead man than to take responsibility for unwise, hasty decisions.

Acceptance in the case of a terminally ill loved one is also difficult. Again, this is not a state of happiness, it is just a state of awareness of the reality of the impending death, rather than an earlier denial. When my mother finally received the correct diagnosis of Alzheimer's Disease, it was easier to accept her condition. With that acceptance came a sense of relief, of peace. I no longer had to fight against the truth, trying to find a cure for her symptoms. I just had to learn to live with it. When I finally stopped praying for a miracle, and started praying for my own strength to help her through the various stages of the disease, I accepted the fact that she would never be the mother I once knew and that eventually she would die.

Accepting Jennie's death as a reality was much more difficult since there was no body for proof. I gained a great appreciation for the overwhelming pain that parents of lost children must endure. Recently, however, a teenager who does not live far from my house, as the crow flies, so to speak, was cited for killing and burying a neighbor's dog. According to where Jennie was last seen, she in all probability ended up near this boy's home. She had never left the immediate area in front of our house (except for one excursion as a puppy), but there is a first time for everything. Believing Jennie died quickly from a gunshot has somehow eased the fear and pain of not knowing what happened and has helped me to accept the fact that she will never come home.

Nevertheless, there was always that little thread of hope that runs through the whole grief process, especially when associated with someone who is dying. It left the door open to the possibility that someone took Jennie in, fed her, and loved her, just as I had always hoped there would be a cure for Alzheimer's, or that there would be a miracle, or perhaps even that mother had been misdiagnosed and eventually the right diagnosis could be treated with medicine, even though I knew it was just wishful thinking. What is life without hope? More importantly, how could we face death without hope?

Accepting the death of a loved one is not an end to grief. We must move beyond the loss, not just to accept it, but to find meaning from it to incorporate into a new life. It is strange how much easier it was to see beyond the losses encountered by my friends and family than it was to find meaning from my own. My married life had been almost perfect, especially the last few years with the children grown, grandchildren to enjoy, and a new freedom to enjoy each other free from the daily schedules of growing, active children. We had always kept the romance alive and our love had matured and deepened through the years. Financially we were more secure than we had ever been and it was fun for me to pass on the rewards to the children and grandchildren. Suddenly, my near perfect world was shattered. How does one get beyond that?

Nevertheless, from the very beginning, I was able to see my situation from the perspective of other widows. When I thought how difficult it was for me to be without my husband, I would think how fortunate I was not to be left with young children to raise by myself or how difficult it would be to be retired and have twenty-four hours a day, seven days a week to fill the void. At least I was still working to keep me busy and to make me tired, tired enough at the end of the day so that not fixing supper for two was more of a relief than a regret. Although it is true that some of my tiredness was due to the physical and emotional exhaustion of grief, I adjusted to welcome doing things on my own schedule and energy level without having to consider someone else's. I am not saying that I was glad for the new life, I am just saying that being alone with no responsibilities for anyone but myself after standing on my feet all day is a lot different than being alone all evening after being alone all day.

At any rate, it was small bits like this of rationalizing my loss by comparing it to others that eventually helped me look at my life and say, "I can go on." Just how I would manage, or where my life would lead me, I was not sure, but I knew I had to pick up the pieces and keep going. I knew my life would be very different, not just because my world had changed, but because I had changed. We cannot experience the deep reality of grief and emerge as the same person we were before. We either become bitter or more compassionate and understanding with a strong desire to turn the loss into a meaningful experience. In some way, it is affirming that there was meaning in the life of the departed loved one, and in another way, it is an acknowledgment of gratitude that you are not the one who died, that your life must have some value because you are still alive, and that you are going to make every minute of that life count. It is the realization that life is a precious gift, however temporary, to be lived with meaning and love. It is transcendence, rising above our tragedies, not forgetting them, but gaining new strength to turn them from something negative into something positive.

At first, I could not seem to concentrate on anything for any length of time after my husband died. Normally a person who cannot sit and relax without keeping my hands busy by knitting, crocheting, or other handcrafting, I had no initiative or desire to work on anything. I was too restless even to watch a complete show on television, often using the dreaded remote control to switch channels in order to watch two or three shows at the same time. As time went by, I watched more and more movies, using them as an escape from the reality of my own life. When my husband was alive, I rarely watched movies — much to his chagrin. Of course that was partly due to the fact that he liked war movies and I already knew who won the war!

I used to be so upset when my husband would continually change the channel with the remote control. He always left it on a station just long enough to raise my curiosity as to what would happen next, then in a flash there was an altogether different show with different characters. I considered flipping through channels a "male thing" but I soon became very adept at it myself. What was I doing? I kept telling myself I had to do something with my life. However, I just sat on the corner of the couch with the remote control pointed at the television.

With the first anniversary of my husband's death inspiring me to write a general poem of comfort instead of poems for specific people with personal references, and Jennie's disappearance compelling me to write a personal memoir, I began a journey to bring meaning back into my life, and to give meaning to my husband's death. Neither of us had finished college and it was a regret that we both shared. When I finished writing the rough draft of my memoir, my lack of formal education made me feel inadequate for writing any material that might eventually be published. So, at age fifty, through a series of events which seemed almost pre-ordained, I enrolled in a program at Vermont College of Norwich University to gain new skills, ideas, and perspectives. Returning to an academic climate put my husband's death into a new perspective. I would never have gone back for my degree if he were still alive, nor would I have written the hymn and a rough draft of a manu-script. My life is constantly opening up to new possibilities that never would have interested me before. My husband's life and love are treasured gifts, but his death was not the end of his gifts. He has made it possible for me to grow spiritually and intellectually, see-ing the world with a new vision for myself and humanity. It was my big step in healing my grief and transcending my losses. In the words of Ashley Prend,

> Transcending the loss is about striving to make the ex-perience an ultimately positive and redemptive one, it is about grievers resolved to using their pain in a mean-ingful and inspirational way. Transcending loss, then, refers to those who have made the best of a terrible situation and have let grief teach them important les-sons about life. It refers to those who insist that some-thing tragic can and will lead to something meaning-ful. Those grievers have discovered the gifts that flow from grief.

My journey through the aspects and emotions of grief would not be complete without mentioning the fact that it is possible to grieve without acceptance or moving beyond our losses. It is not always automatic that our emotions come to the surface to eventu-ally be released. They often get buried or denied. Trying to avoid grief or staying locked in its emotions only leads to complications both physically and psychologically.

I have had my own learning experience with unresolved grief. It was not after a loss from death, but rather the sudden break-up, my first year in college, of a four-year teen-age relationship. We had gone to separate colleges in different states so I am sure a break-up was inevitable, but the circumstances were abrupt and unique. There was no argument, no discussion, in effect, no closure. His friend came to my dorm one day and told me through his own tears that the young man who I thought I would marry some day had left college to marry someone else. How could this be? We had just talked on the phone a few days before and everything seemed fine. Too proud to cry, and too concerned for the emotions of the bearer of the bad tidings, I could not admit that my world had been destroyed. It was a loss which should have had a grieving period, but what did I know about grief as a freshman in college? I did not experience any stage of grief, not even anger. I went on as if it did not matter, but it did. I suppose, technically, I was in the state of shock and never moved away from it.

A year later, I was in trouble. I could not sleep. I did not eat. I could hardly put one foot in front of the other. I used deodorant for hair spray, or vise-versa, and the inner layers of my skin felt as if they were alive. Occasionally, I would throw something across the room to release the terrible feeling of agitated nerve endings.

One weekend, a friend convinced me to go home so she could stay at my parents' house in order for her to spend some time with her boyfriend who attended the college in my hometown. As we walked through the door, I collapsed. My muscles would no longer function. I could not even control my facial muscles to form words. It was the most frightening experience I have ever been through. My unresolved grief had manifested itself in full force with an emotional breakdown.

In retrospect, this was one of the best learning experiences of my life. I vowed that no man was worth my sanity and I gained a greater appreciation of my own self-worth. Through an unlikely savior, I was loaned a book by Norman Vincent Peale during my recovery containing the Serenity Prayer that somehow leapt out of the pages to become my philosophy of life and my reference on how to handle everyday situations that arise in business and bringing up a family. Losing my dependent nature gave my marriage more stability, love, and mutual respect than I ever thought to be humanly possible. It also gave me my first awakening to a spiritual experience with the reality of a Force in my life greater than my own. (By the way, the young man returned to college to become a lawyer, is still married to the same person, moved back to our hometown just nine miles away, and on the rare occasions when we run into each other, the past is never the present.) I am very grateful for the personal strength I gained and for the positive effect the experience had in shaping my personality and my spirituality. Which, of course, is another example of transcendence, even if it came from deeply buried emotions.

Grief is painful and lonely. Lonely because no one can go through it for us. Others can help, for sure, but in the end it is up to the individual to experience the intense, agonizing emotions of grief, to work through them, to move beyond them, to find meaning in his or her life and the lives of departed loved ones. At first it may seem an impossible task and yet, although it cannot be accomplished overnight, healing from grief can take us to places deep within ourselves that we never knew existed and we can emerge with more sensitivity, spirituality, and inner strength. We can survive, we can live and love again.

This Grief Is Mine

This grief is mine —
No way to share it as in days gone by
    with birthday toys,
    hand-me-down clothes,
    and childhood joys.
These tears are all mine alone to cry.

This grief is mine —
And though I keep it safely tucked inside,
    when friends go home,
    the family leaves,
    and I'm alone,
The pain within will no longer hide.

This grief is mine —
When nighttime arrives , on my bed I lay
    with pain so deep
    my body aches;
    I cannot sleep.
When morning breaks, I must face the day.

This grief is mine —
When fond memories stir within my heart
    of days gone by,
    cherished moments
    make me ask "Why?"
Then lost hopes and dreams make my tears start.

I cannot see beyond today's grey skies,
    but time, they say,
    will dry my tears,
    take pain away,
And give my life new meaning and ties.

Yes, healing will come in the course of time,
the pain will fade,
the tears will cease,
a new life made,
But, there is no end for this grief of mine.

Chapter Two

Grief Before Death: When Someone Is Dying

Grief is not reserved for death; it is a very real experience for those who are terminally ill and their loved ones, working their way from the shock of the actual diagnosis, through denial, anger, bargaining, depression, and all the other emotions of grief until finally some form of acceptance is attained. Yet, even when the impending death is accepted as a certainty, there is always the hope of a last minute cure or miracle which buffers the trauma of knowing someone is about to die.

It is very difficult to deal emotionally with the impending death of a loved one. We deny that death is a certainty, we are angry that our loved one contracted the disease in the first place, we feel helpless and at the same time guilty that we cannot stop or reverse the progression of the disease. One of my friends felt guilty because when death was near for her mother, she could not get her to eat. She thought it was somehow her fault and if only she could get her to eat, everything would be alright. Not only do we have to come to terms with our own emotions, but we also must deal with the grieving process of the one who is dying. And with the individual aspect of grief, we are not going through the same emotions at the same time nor in the same way.

How we react to our emotions can affect the dying process of our loved one. For instance, if he or she reaches acceptance before we do, our reluctance can send them a message that we want them to fight to live, making them feel guilty for leaving us. Elisabeth Kübler-Ross addresses the idea of wanting our loved ones to be strong by saying the family "may encourage the fight for life to the end, and they may implicitly communicate that accepting one's end is regarded as a cowardly giving up, as a deceit or, even worse yet, a rejection of the family." Accepting one's death does not mean he or she *wants* to leave the family and placing that guilt on our loved one because we are not ready to have them die makes the dying process more difficult.

The guilt for leaving loved ones behind can exist even if we have not demanded that our loved one "hang on," fighting death to the last breath. I remember visiting my friend's mother as she lay dying, yet clinging to life for all she was worth. She had been living with her daughter for many years, participating in the family life, helping with the household chores, and caring for the grandchildren. She was involved with every aspect of their lives, openly and willingly sharing her love, talents, and time. And the feeling was mutual. The family shared their lives with her in an open relationship of love and respect.

She had been a special part of my life too, and as I held her hand and talked to her during one of my last visits, I was suddenly aware that her will to live went far beyond any fear of dying or desire to live on for herself. She was, in fact, unable to leave her family whom she thought still needed her more than she needed to die. And why not? Her family had always made her feel loved and needed which never changed with age or time. Wouldn't they need her forever? The guilt she felt for leaving them was overpowering.

After not eating for days, she slipped into a coma and, as I visited one more time to say my good-byes, my friend and I talked about her mother's feelings. She was aware of her desperate need to cling to life for the family's sake. When her mother died a few days later, she did so with my friend's permission. She told her over and over that it was alright to die and reassured her that the family would be able to get along without her. Helping a loved one die by letting go is not easy for all of us. We sometimes react as movie scenes so often depict as we cry out, "Don't you die on me, I won't let you die."

Letting go is our acceptance of the eventual death. It is giving permission to our loved one not only to die, but to live their last days as they wish. It is often easy to take over, making decisions without consulting our loved one's opinion or desire. As Mary Jones writes in her book, *Secret Flowers,* "It is difficult to let another person live their own life, far harder to let them die in their own way." We become experts at knowing what is best. And one of the things we seem to dwell upon is eating. It seems that our obsession with food in the United States is always with us. Marrying into an Italian family, I have come to realize that food is a form of communication as well as performing social and nutritional functions! At any rate, when a friend's father was dying from cancer, she would often express her annoyance at his lack of desire to eat and especially to drink enough water. In her mind, he should be concerned with taking care of himself nutritionally. What for? Is eating a cure for advanced cancer? Does cleaning your plate improve the quality of dying? If one is not hungry and has no urge to eat because the body is beginning to shut down preparing itself to die, who are we to judge how much food or water should be ingested. To me, trying to force someone to eat is like saying, "You may be dying, but you are going to die healthy!"

I think as we become caretakers for someone who is terminally ill we often forget that the person who is dying is still a viable person with thoughts and feelings of his or her own. I have seen many family members treat their dying loved one as a young child, incapable of functioning on an adult level. I have even heard friends and family members talk in front of their loved one as if he or she were not able to hear or comprehend what is being said. Perhaps it is our way of breaking away, severing ties before death, but it is not taking into consideration the dying process for our loved one. Even though they are doing their own breaking away, they still need to feel a part of life around them on their own terms, not ours.

To some extent it is different when a person, such as my mother, has a disease that affects the normal functioning of the brain. I fought valiantly to delay a role-reversal that was eventually inevitable. I had always respected her mental capacity, which was far above my own, and having to take over to make her decisions was the hardest thing I ever did during her illness. However, when I finally accepted the change, I went too far, sometimes forgetting that she still was an adult. Looking back, I think I made her my child not just by my actions, but in my mind. It seemed to make it easier for me to care for her without harboring any hard feelings. Whether it was easier for her, I will never know. It just happened.

One of the best things we can do for our loved one who is dying is to listen to them. Whether he or she wants to talk about concerns, or fears, hopes or dreams, or perhaps regrets, the feelings and emotions of grief are as great as our own. It is just as important to bring those emotions to the surface as it would be for any person who is grieving. Burying emotions deep inside ourselves or simply denying their existence does more harm than good.

The regrets I have over the way I handled my mother's illness stem from my taking control and not listening or considering her feelings. From the time she was first diagnosed until she died, I never talked about the disease in front of her, never mind *with* her. In her more rational moments, however brief they were, I visited with her as if nothing was wrong, never allowing her an opportunity to express her fears or discuss any emotions, assuming that she could not grasp what was happening to her. How I wish I had just asked her what she was feeling or if she had any questions. I know now, there were times when I could have listened, but I talked instead. She knew she was different than she had been and, in her frustration, she shed tears, tears that I wiped away but avoided the feelings behind them.

Often when someone is dying, there is a family member or friend who will not visit that person in the final stages of the illness because it is too difficult to bear, not wanting to remember him or her in such a weakened condition but rather as healthy, before the terminal illness took over the body and/or the mind. Sometimes our inability to cope with the last stages of dying is our feeling of helplessness as to what to do or what to say, when all we have to do is listen.

Another factor that makes us uncomfortable is visualizing our own eventual death; in our fear of possibly experiencing the same suffering, we cannot cope with seeing our loved one withering away. I think our fears of what might happen to us are worse than when they become a reality. I remember when my neighbor developed Alzheimer's and her daughter moved back home to care for her. As the disease progressed, I used to view the things she did for her mother with an adamant assertion that I could *never* do the same if I was put in the same position. The strange thing was that when my own mother became ill with Alzheimer's, things I watched my neighbor's daughter do that I just knew I could never do, such as taking her mother to a public restaurant, paled in comparison to what I actually had to do and did willfully, such as cleaning her up after a bout with diarrhea for which she had no understanding of what was happening to her. Taking my mother to restaurants or out for ice cream was easy. Giving her a change of scenery and seeing her happy to be out, far outweighed any embarrassment I might feel if she stuffed the food in her cheeks or used her fingers instead of utensils. I will say, however, that there were only a few restaurants where I felt comfortable taking her, and most of them were fast-food restaurants—but not all. Nevertheless, I did take her often as it was one thing we could still do together.

So many people feel that Alzheimer's places its victims in a state of euphoria, believing the old adage, "Ignorance is bliss." I know this is not true. My mother had many fears and frustrations until the very last stages of her illness. She was often aware that people treated her differently and referred to a time "when I was well" as a better time. I knew all this, and yet I still tried to protect her feelings by ignoring them. Getting Alzheimer's was the only thing I ever remember my mother being afraid of, or at least ever expressing that fear. She often played the piano at the local nursing home on Fridays for a sing-a-long gathering of the residents. One of the residents was the husband of a good friend. He had Alzheimer's and every weekend she would always say the same thing. "If I ever get that disease, I hope you will take me out and shoot me." By the time he died, my mother was already well into the beginning stages of the disease.

In not wanting to upset her by frankly discussing her disease, I helped imprison her in an emotional silence. Perhaps I thought I was protecting her, or assuming she had already lost all comprehension of what was happening to her. Or perhaps in reality, I was protecting my own emotions from exposure.

Whatever I was protecting, I guess I could say it did not work on either level. The emotional roller-coaster of grief either before or after death produces emotions that come in waves — not ripples on a pond, but tidal waves in the ocean — and there is no controlling feelings that surface without warning, changing with the wind. Feelings swing from praying your loved one will not die, to hoping for a miracle, to wishing for death to end the suffering. And with that wish comes guilt as you contemplate whose suffering you want to end — yours or your loved one's. Whether it is physical pain or mental anguish, it is difficult to watch a loved one reduced to living a lifeless life. But it is a part of life and death and, more importantly, love. Being open to a dying loved one's needs, wishes, and fears will help heal our own grief. It directs our grief into a positive action rather than a negative feeling. For in helping others, no matter what the circumstance, we always help ourselves.

Experts in the field of grief counseling tell us that knowing someone is going to die affects the amount of time in our own grieving process after a death. As we begin grieving before the death, we actually start breaking our ties and letting go so that when death comes we heal faster than after a sudden death. I have experienced both types of death, both sudden and lingering, and I find that I cannot make a judgment as to which one needed more time to come to terms with. When someone dies suddenly, there are no tormenting memories of the suffering, of a loved one changing in looks, behavior, or mental ability. You always see your loved one in your mind as he or she was just before the death. When a person suffers from a terminal illness, the memories are more haunting. When I think of my husband, I see happy times, a handsome man, a healthy man. When I think of my mother, I see blank stares, a shriveled body, a helpless woman. It is often hard to bring up mental pictures of her before her illness. And to me, the healing process from grief is dependent on how we perceive our memories of a loved one. I think it is easier to overcome grief when you can cherish the good memories than when you harbor bad ones due to suffering. I cannot count how many times I responded with gratitude to people's concern for me after my husband's death with, "At least he did not have to suffer."

Another factor in my questioning of one grief process lasting longer than another due to the length of time we have prior knowledge of the death is the emotional bond that is formed by tending to someone's needs day after day. The more you are needed, the stronger the bond. This is true with parents and their babies, with parents and children with serious illness, and with parents and children with emotional problems. I am not saying that a parent *loves* a baby, an emotional child, or a sickly child more than his or her siblings. I am saying that the pull on their emotions is stronger and therefore the emotional bond is stronger. At least that is how I see it from my own experience as a child and again as a parent, but that is another story. For now, I am just saying that by the time my mother died, there was an emotional attachment that went way beyond my love for her. Not being needed by her any more after her death was as hard to deal with as my losing her.

The one thing a terminal illness permits that sudden death does not is a chance to say good-bye and perhaps to put into words the love we feel for our loved one and how grateful we are that he or she was a part of our lives. A sudden death does not allow that and it is one of the major regrets we have as we begin our grief. "I never got a chance to say good-bye." This is fact we might all do well to remember and tell those we love how we feel every chance we get, just in case we do not get that one last chance.

Before You Go

Am I doing enough to help you
With the things I say and do?
Is it easier for you in any way
Because of something I did today?
Please squeeze my hand if you can tell
I would do anything to make you well.
Your gentle kiss when I was small
Relieved the pain when I would fall
And dried my tears when things went wrong.
How could something so gentle be so strong?
I wish I could kiss away your tears
And help erase all your fears,
But all I can give are love and prayer
To show how much I really care.
I wish my love could make you whole,
For I love you with all my heart and soul.
But love is not a magic wand
No matter how strong is the bond,
And you must know before you die
The bond between us will never untie.
It will go with you in eternal peace,
It will stay with me and never cease.
For worldly things will come and go,
But love remains forever so.

The Heart Remembers

I do not feel hurt or angry
    Because you no longer know my name.
It does not seem to matter
    For I know you are not to blame.

I know if it were possible
    You would definitely recall
The special memories between us
    And the love running through them all.

From childhood days of following you
    Around the breakfast table each day,
Drinking orange juice from every glass
    That you just filled along the way.

To grown-up days and wedding plans
    About to turn my life upside down.
I curled up in your lap once more
    The night before I wore your wedding gown.

Your mind may not remember
    All the memories that we share,
But your heart has not forgotten
    And you keep them forever there.

So, when someone will ask me
    How I cope with your rejection,
I simply say your mind may be blank
    But your heart has perfect recollection.

Watch And Wait

Watching and waiting. Waiting and watching.
It is so hard to watch you die —
harder still to wait for death.
I feel helpless.
Every day there are changes —
changes that bring you closer to death,
taking you farther away from me.
I try to remember the way you were
before this nightmare began.
Sometimes I can't and it frightens me.
If only I could wake up;
If only you would die.
Either way the nightmare might end —
or would it just begin?
I am not ready to know.
It is better to watch and wait.

Are You Still In There?

Mother, are you still in there
    behind that cold blank stare?
Is there any understanding
    when I say how much I care?

Mother, are you still in there
    behind that senseless chatter?
Are you trying somehow to tell me
    how much I really matter?

Mother, are you still in there
    behind your tight-clenched fist?
Do you have any awareness
    of how very much you are missed?

Each night I go to bed and pray
    for mercy or for a miracle, too.
Then I wonder who needs them more;
    could it be me instead of you?

One thing I know for certain;
    there is nothing to compare
With the torment deep inside my heart
    when I pray you are not there.

The Roller Coaster

The news deals a crushing blow.
We plunge head-first into a deep ravine of despair.
    Fear, anguish, anxiety race within,
    tears, unanswered questions race without.
Spiraling downward, we near the lowest level
    only to be pulled upward —
slowly at first, then more quickly, rising
    to a new height of hope.
As our ascent begins to level, we catch our breath
    just before we are pushed to the edge
    and hurled over it,
    descending to a new low.
We are afraid to look down too far
    for it is so steep.
Without touching the bottom, new hope suddenly
    skyrockets us to its highest point.
The acceleration leaves us breathless —
    for just a moment
    before plummeting
    far below
    into the unknown.

I will never ride a roller coaster again.

Chapter Three

Loss Of A Pet

As children, one of the first losses we might encounter is the loss of a pet. Whether that pet is a turtle, a fish, a rabbit, a dog, a cat, a farm animal, or any other animal, attachments to pets can be very strong, causing great sorrow when they die. For many children, the death of a pet is their first glimpse into the reality that life is not forever — not for animals or for people. It is quite a concept for a child to comprehend.

I often wonder if some of the fatal shootings and murders committed by children are a result of watching cartoon characters and real actors die on television shows only to reappear healthy and vibrant on another show, leaving a child with absolutely no perception of the finality of death. A child who loses a pet is forced to confront that finality. Depending on the relationship between the child and his or her pet, its death can produce feelings of sadness to feelings of deep sorrow. Children experience grief and its emotions just as adults do. It is something that we cannot protect or shield them from. Denying a child's grief is as unhealthy for him or her as denying our own grief.

There are many things we can do to help children deal with their grief. Letting them cry without fear of embarrassment or guilt, letting them talk about their loss and their feelings, or helping them turn their feelings into something creative such as writing or art are all positive ways to help children deal with the many emotions of grief. Virginia Fry, a grief therapist who works with children, is an advocate of using the creative arts as healing tools. Speaking to children and adults as well, Fry says, "We never get a choice about who will die in our lives. But we do get to choose what to do with our memories. By using our memories to make poetry, drawings, and stories, we create a truth we can live with."

Make no mistake, I am not trying to say that children are the only ones who grieve when a pet dies. I am merely pointing out that since a pet's life span is much shorter than a human's, the odds are that a child will see a family pet die before experiencing the death of a sibling, a parent, a friend, or even a grandparent. Nevertheless, adults form strong attachments to pets as well, and often experience as much deep-seated grief as with the death of a cherished friend.

I am one of those adults who form strong attachments to animals and who grieves deeply when they die. Perhaps it is because I was always the one to feed them, tend to their needs, and care for them when they were sick. There is an unconditional love between pets and people, a love which people need as much as the pets depend on it for survival. I have read many times recently how pets promote good health, both physical and emotional, especially for people living alone and for the elderly. Nursing homes, such as the one where my father-in-law stayed for a while after his hospitalization from a rare form of meningitis, often have an "in-house" pet for their residents. The bond that develops between people and pets and even the act of petting are both therapeutic. When that bond is broken by death, the grief can be overwhelming. To minimize those feelings of sorrow is a mistake. The grief suffered at the death of a pet is very real; as with all grief, it takes time to heal.

I had grown up with family dogs as house pets, but my husband grew up with hunting dogs which were kept outside. It was an ongoing discussion of where the dog would stay if and when we got one. When he finally brought home a little beagle puppy, it was late October and the weather was already quite cold. We made a barricade for the kitchen and my husband consented to letting the puppy stay in the kitchen until spring when she would be old enough to stay outside. Obviously spring never came because not even a day had gone by before my husband carried the puppy (Penny) into the living room and from that day on, home to Penny became anywhere she wanted to be — except our bed — at least until after my husband went to work. Her favorite place to sleep was with our oldest son who immediately gave up his security blanket in favor of a warm, cuddly puppy.

We all adored her as she was a good pet and a great rabbit dog. When the boys were sick, she kept a vigil by them until they were well enough to run and play again. Both boys shot their first rabbits in front of her. As she got older, my husband decided to get another puppy to train with Penny while she was still running well. But Penny's cancer and the new puppy arrived at about the same time. Penny's death was hard for all of us, but I took it a step further by blaming the new puppy. She would never replace Penny and I wanted no part of her. I did not completely ignore her, I just did not feel the same bond as I had with Penny.

Then one day, the new dog, Suzie, was attacked by two coyotes. She was a mess, but we made the decision to try and save her. Two hundred stitches later, Suzie was near death. The veterinarian called and asked if I could come and sit with her for a while. She must have felt abandoned after her ordeal to be left in a strange cage with none of her family around and was in the process of giving up. However, when she saw me, her eyes lit up and she picked her head up for the first time. Somewhere between those first few moments at the vets, and weeks of bathing and applying salve on her wounds, Suzie and I formed that missing bond of unconditional love. I did not care what she looked like with all her ugly wounds, and she let me perform my nursing duties without any resistance, as if she knew I was helping her to heal.

I am not sure we did her any favors by deciding to save her, but she gained a few years, running rabbits as well as ever, although she had continually recurring abscesses on many of her old wounds. Antibiotics and salves became a routine, cementing the bond between us until the night we arrived home from a party to find her dead. There was no indication earlier in the day that she was any different, and seeing her lying still was a shock for us.

The boys were both gone from the house by then; only our daughter was still at home to mourn the loss. It took my husband several weeks before he could come to terms with his grief, even having to call a friend to help him dispose of Suzie's body as he could not bring himself to do it. As for me, the emotional attachment of caring for her left me with an emptiness that lasted long after the sadness and tears.

As difficult as it was to lose our first two beagles, none was more traumatic than the disappearance of our third and final one.

She was the youngest, only four when she disappeared. You might think the emotional attachment would not be as strong as the relationship built up in the years of each of the other two, but it was much deeper. Perhaps it was because Jenny was filling our empty nest, perhaps it was her personality or her excellent nose for rabbits, or perhaps it was just her need and ours to be loved and needed, but she took over our house and our hearts — and our bed!

When my husband died, Jenny became my sounding board for all my thoughts and fears. She always greeted me at the door with wiggles and squeals of enthusiasm whether I was gone for five minutes or five hours, and she kept a vigil on my emotional roller-coaster, just as Penny had kept watch over my children. The hardest part of reconciling myself to Jenny's death is the not knowing what happened or where her body is. It is a nagging unresolved mystery that still comes back to haunt me even now. It would have been easier to have closure to my grief if I had a body to bury or at least some answers, and I saw a glimpse of the trauma that parents must feel when a child is missing. Even with weeks of searching, posters placed in local stores, ads in newspapers and on the radio, I still wonder if I could have done more or if I gave up too soon. But as with any disappearance, coming to terms with it does not mean that I ever stopped glancing at ads from the Humane Society to see if the description of any beagle would fit Jenny's size and age even though now I have to add four years.

I like to think that Jenny and my husband are together again, chasing rabbits that cannot die through heavenly forests filled with wildlife co-existing in harmony. After all, according to Richard Matheson in *What Dreams May Come,* my dream of what heaven is like may be my reality in heaven. And as I always say, if you are going to dream, you might as well dream big or, in this case, dream what you want to be so. Dreams and happy memories bring peace and comfort to a grieving soul.

Penny

My heart is very heavy
  As I think of you tonight
And all the things you were to us
  Keep coming into light.

You were a friend to all of us
  And could sense our every mood.
You even came to my crazy whistle
  Because you thought it might mean food.

You laid beside the children
  When they were feeling sick,
And could seem to make them better
  With just one gentle lick.

You did not even play favorites
  But would sleep with them all,
And seemed to know whose turn it was
  Even if the wrong one would call.

And in the woods where you loved to be,
  No other dog could compare
To the hunting skills and comradery
  That you and Glenn did share.

But I guess that I will miss you most
  Because of the time that was so dear,
When you would crawl in beside me,
  The minute Glenn was not near.

And if there is a doggy heaven,
  I can tell you just one thing,
They have got the best dog today
  That anyone will ever bring.

Suzie

At first, I blamed you for Penny's death
  Getting us off to a tenuous start.
Now that wasted time in our friendship
  Only adds to the emptiness in my heart.

I guess we did not do you any favors
  When we decided to save your life.
The last few years were a constant struggle,
  As open sores filled your days with strife.

You never seemed to show your pain,
  As you let me salve your sores with ease.
Strengthening the bond between us
  After that attack by the coyotes.

Your bravery was not the only reason
  You eventually won over my heart.
Your willingness to please, your trusting eyes,
  And your unconditional love played their part.

So, it is with love I say good-bye to you
  With regret for my delayed acceptance.
Yet I know the bond we developed through caring
  By far, holds the greater significance.

Fall Memories

Vibrant crimsons turn to bronze and soon the trees stand naked.
The ground becomes dressed with a coat of many colors,
finally losing its beauty to a dryness, turning the cover
into a lifeless accumulation of debris,
signaling the onset of raking.
With each rustle, I am pulled back to another time
where memories run sweeter. Seeing two friends
jumping in the leaves brings a smile
as they frolic like children.
Around in circles they race until the right moment
finds them spreading all four legs like eagles' wings
as they soar onto the highest mountain of leaves,
sinking to its depth as if entering a crater.
Leaves scatter under their feet as they quickly bounce
back on all fours, ready for more runs
and more flights converging onto cushioned landings.
The impressions of playful bodies in the leaves
are now just impressions in my mind.
And now the rustle only echos the crackling sound of flying paws,
breaking the silence, breaking the heart, changing my smile to a
tear.

Chapter Four

Losing Grandparents

If losing a pet is one of the first deaths we may experience in our lives, then losing a grandparent is even more likely to be a first loss as we all have grandparents, but we do not all have pets. In an unwritten law of nature, it is expected that grandparents should and will die before parents, siblings, and friends. However, knowing our grandparents will die someday does not make their deaths any easier to bear.

There is a special bond between a grandparent and a grandchild. Perhaps it is due somewhat to the fact that grandparents do not have the day-to-day responsibilities of raising the grandchildren and are therefore more tolerant toward their faults and misbehavior, or perhaps it is due partly to the fact that grandparents simply have more time to devote to the grandchildren when they are together. I am sure everyone can think of many reasons why the relationship between grandparent and grandchild is different than that of the parents and child. As a grandparent myself, I often adhere to the familiar idea that if I had known how much fun it was to have grandchildren, I would have skipped having the children first which, of course, is neither possible nor true. Actually, I was one of those mothers who enjoyed every stage of her children's lives — including the teens.

The point is, however, there is an unconditional love for a grandchild and the same is true in reverse — a child loves a grandparent unconditionally. I am sure there are exceptions to this ideal relationship, but usually when a grandparent dies, a child loses one of his or her best friends. I recently read where a grandmother served as matron of honor at her granddaughter's wedding. The bride's reason for choosing her grandmother was to follow tradition and have her best friend be her attendant. Her grandmother had been her best friend all her life. What a tribute!

After my husband died, my then eight-year-old granddaughter was given an assignment to write a song. She wrote a poem about her close friend, her grandfather. Her poem is included in the poems at the end of this chapter.

The bond between grandparent and grandchild is undoubtedly stronger if they live near to one another than if they live miles apart. Day-to-day or week-to-week interaction builds a familiarity of likes and dislikes, friends and activities, etc., that is not possible to develop in yearly or bi-yearly visits. Yet, even when distance prohibits frequent visits, there is still a relationship that is unique and deep. When a grandparent dies, children of all ages grieve.

Their grief should not be overlooked or dismissed lightly. Their emotions are strong and need to be addressed. Trying to protect them by keeping them away from funerals or away from conversations concerning the death of their grandparent is more harmful than helpful. Just as the funeral preparations and services provide closure for adults, they also help children deal with their loss. Not that you should force a child to take part, but if he or she wants to, that need should not be denied. There is no need to shield them by acting as if there is nothing wrong. They *know* there is something wrong. They have lost a great deal more than just a member of the older generation they have lost a refuge, a never-ending source of wisdom, an enveloping love, a friend, and for some, an unlimited supply of gifts and money.

I was ten years old when my paternal grandfather died. Although my maternal grandmother died first, my grandfather's death was the first death I can remember, as I was only two years old when my grandmother died and I have no conscious memory of her. Both sets of grandparents lived in Massachusetts while we lived in Vermont, but we made frequent visits, especially to see my father's parents. Dad was an only child and, being close to his parents, he went often to help his aging parents. My grandfather was a very kind man, soft spoken, and with a gentle nature. His eyes could draw you right into their warmth. He loved my sister and me without reservation. We used to sit on his lap, follow him everywhere, and go with him for rides in his car. I loved being in his garden with him. It was immaculately cared for with flowers, fruit trees, and my favorite arbor. Neatly trimmed hedges surrounded both the garden and the house. My most favorite memory, however, is my grandfather's old car. I am not sure why I enjoyed being in his car, but I can still smell its interior today.

My grandfather had respiratory problems which undoubtedly were the result of too much smoking. As his health declined, so did our time with him. We still visited as often, but my grandmother made sure my sister and I did not disturb him. She did not possess my grandfather's kind and gentle ways. She was abrupt and aloof, not with meanness, but rather just a lack of warmth. When my grandfather died, his house became a cold silent tomb, and empty — definitely empty.

Whether or not my sister and I went to the calling hours and the funeral was not an option for us as we had nowhere else to stay during the services. Seeing my grandfather lying in a casket is still a very vivid memory for me as it was the first time I had ever been exposed to funeral rituals. For years I resented the fact that my last image of my grandfather was one of lying in a casket. Yet, by the same token, I would have felt worse if my parents had just told me he was dead and I had never seen him again. I think as a ten-year-old, I needed to see him in order to understand that he did not just vanish. The main thing was that I was not afraid to see him, and I think that death should be something that children are taught not to fear or to be uncomfortable in its presence.

After my grandfather died, my grandmother came to live with us. I admit she spoiled me as she insisted on doing all the little household chores that I should have been doing to help my mother since she worked out as treasurer of a local bank. Grandma washed dishes, dusted, did the baking, and helped with the meals. She needed to feel useful and who was I to argue? I would like to be able to say that living with her brought a new closeness to our relationship, but I cannot. However, it did provide more of an understanding and awareness of who she was as a person, thus enabling me to see beyond her reservedness to realize that she loved us in the only way she knew how to love. And I loved her in the only way she would accept my love. She lived with us but did not participate in family life, she loved us but was not loving, she gave but was not giving.

I was in college when she died. Despite her rigid personality, I missed her terribly. She had been in the hospital and I had just left her room about twenty minutes before she died. I was home for the holidays and the hospital was on my way to a high school basketball game. I wish I had just stayed with her a little longer, but perhaps it was best for her to die as she had lived, just out of the reach of those she loved.

My maternal grandfather has always been a model for me of a perfect man. He was tall and handsome, with a quiet strength, full of warmth and compassion, understanding and wisdom. He was a religious man and lived his faith with conviction. He took in his sister-in-law and her family when they needed a home, and cared for my aunt and her daughter after her divorce, assuming the role of a father to my cousin. They had a close relationship and I often envied the fact that they were together so much while I could only be with my grandfather for short visits.

Although he made several trips a year to Vermont to spend time with us, the majority of our time in Massachusetts was spent with my father's parents with only a few days reserved for my mother's family. It just did not seem fair to me as a child that my cousin was with him so much because, on top of all his other attributes, my grandfather was fun to be with. He liked to play games, put together puzzles, go for rides, go to amusement parks, and he had a subtle but great sense of humor. He was also a dedicated employee, keeping the books for a large bakery until just before he died at he age of 79. But his best attribute as a grandfather was his willingness to spoil me. That's what grandparents do the best, and he did it very well! His method? Why, it was butter, of course. Mother never bought butter; she always used margarine. My grandfather knew how much I liked the real butter that his sister churned on her farm and he never made a trip to Vermont without bringing some butter for me.

He died right after I was married. We all mourned his death with great sorrow. But instead of envy for my cousin, I now grieved for her as well for she had lost so much more than a grandfather.

She lost the only father-figure she had ever known, she lost her confidant, she lost her best friend. I will never know how she managed to sing a solo at his funeral with such a clear and beautiful voice when her heart was so heavy with grief. It was such a tribute to their relationship. It will always remain my favorite memory of her and of her love and devotion for our grandfather.

Funeral rites and rituals provide a certain sense of closure as well as comfort for those who grieve the loss of a loved one. My sister could not attend my grandfather's funeral, and her grief overwhelmed her. Thirty-two years later, she still harbors a feeling of incompleteness and regret when she thinks of him. For me, I feel sad that my children never knew him.

Perhaps the death of a grandparent which gave me the most insight into myself was that of my step-grandmother. My grandfather had remarried several years after his wife died, marrying a woman we all knew. Following our cousin's lead, who I am sure was having a hard time adjusting to another woman in my grandfather's life, my sister and I joined in on giving his new wife a hard time. We teased and tormented her relentlessly. At least that is the way it was at first, but after time, she won us all over with her "grandmotherly" ways. We never called her grandmother, we just added an "aunt" to her first name to show some amount of respect. She died ten years after my grandfather's death. In all the time I knew her, I never really told her how much I loved her as I undoubtedly had never admitted it to myself.

My guilt over my lack of verbal communication, for feelings that I am sure were known anyway, was immeasurable. With regretful thoughts tormenting my mind, I could only quiet them by writing down what I should have said. Writing is such a positive way to release emotions. It has a way of making intangible thoughts into tangible words that can be seen, analyzed, and dealt with. It was such a sense of relief to see the words in black and white, releasing my emotions, not just on paper, but into the realm of beyond. Dwelling on regrets, things we should have done or said or things we wish we had not done or said, is a negative use of our energy. Writing out those regrets helps put them where they belong — in the past.

Since our life span is measured in years, we think of life as starting from birth, going through childhood, becoming an adult, reaching retirement age, and dying when we reach old age, which I have found changes as the years slip by. When I was young, I associated old age with anyone over fifty, increasing each year until now it is at least the late eighties, if not the nineties. Perhaps in ten more years, I will add ten years more. Nevertheless, we expect our grandparents to live to a ripe old age and then die. That is the way the life cycle is supposed to go. If our grandparents follow the expected pattern, we comfort ourselves with the affirmation that they had a good life and the knowledge that no one can live forever. However, grandparents do not always live to an old age. As with any death, the younger the grandparent, the harder the death is to accept.

My husband was 54 when he died, leaving young grandchildren who still saw him as somewhat of a playmate and friend as opposed to seeing him as an elderly man. (Their perception of age is better than mine was as a child. In my defense, my parents greyed early, my husband did not, and only my hairdresser knows what has happened to my hair!) We all expect older people to die; even children are aware of the life cycle. But no one expects death to come early, making it difficult to understand and to come to terms with our grief.

Therefore, our reaction to the death of our grandparents is not only affected by our relationship with them but also by their age at the time of their death. And by the same token, the age of the grandchildren affects their grief at losing a grandparent. A two-year-old will not have the same reaction as a ten-year-old. The same is undoubtedly true for a teenager and a grandchild in his or her twenties or thirties. But there again, so many factors play a part. If the grandparent lives far away, if the grandparent lives nearby or even with the family, if the grandparents take an active part in their grandchildren's lives either by caring for them or by attending their school activities, the relationship between the combined personalities as well as the ages of both grandparent and child are all determining factors in grieving the death of a grandparent.

Grandfather

You stood so very proud and tall;
You were so loving, gentle and kind.
Your family was most important of all,
Always first in heart and mind.

You set and example by your way
Of loving God and home.
A rich tradition for us all today
To take with us wherever we roam.

You taught me the value of the special bond
Between a grandparent and grandchild.
The many memories of which I am fond
In my heart are forever filed.

Unselfish and unconditional love,
You lavished on me without fail.
You brought as much joy as the sun above
When it shines after a storm of hail.

I will never forget the warmth of your smile
Or the strong compassion in your hug,
Or the back roads we traveled mile after mile
Until one of us nudged you with a tug.

You always brought my favorite things
When you would come to call
Puzzles, games, songs to sing,
But the butter was my favorite of all.

Life won't be the same without you,
Not just for me, but for everyone.
Your memory will live on in all we do,
And will not cease when this day is done.

Grandmother

There were not many hugs when I was young
And I never remember sitting on your knee.
In a way you seemed very distant
Yet, I know you felt love for me.

You did not play games or follow me
To my school functions and such
Yet, in your own way you cared for me
And I am sure loved me very much.

The kitchen was yours when you baked
Never passing on any of your secrets.
Perhaps you just did not know how.
I wonder if you ever had any regrets.

Perhaps by having just one child
And because he was a boy,
You never learned the hugs and kisses
Give little girls so much joy.

But I am not complaining
For I never walked out the door
Without some extra spending money
Each time I went to the store!

The Things I Left Unsaid

Your suffering is all over now
    And the pain has gone away;
For God opened up His heavenly doors
    And took you with Him today.

You will live a new life now
    Full of happiness and love;
And one of everlasting peace
    With God in heaven above.

And waiting there to meet you
    Will be loved ones gone before;
And what a joyous reunion for you
    To be with them all once more.

Your new life will be wonderful.
    I believe this with all my heart,
But I cannot keep the tears away,
    As from this life you depart.

For I cry not for your new life
    But for the one you left behind,
And for the things I left unsaid
    Keeping them only in my mind.

You loved me as if I were your own
    And did things for me with ease.
How could I help but love you
    As a grandmother, Aunt Louise?

But, now it is too late to say these things
    But not too late for you to know,
For I will ask God in my prayers tonight
    To tell you I love you so.

So, until the day when I join you
     And share the thoughts that are in my head,
I'll trust in God to tell you
     All the things I left unsaid.

A New Life Is A New Way To Love

The pain has now subsided
      And the worries have all gone,
For Nonny's earthly battle
      Has been elegantly won.

She had a heart as pure as gold
      And lived her life in love.
She certainly has earned a place
      With God in heaven above.

She will soon be with Him
      In a life of love and peace,
And in a new world of beauty
      That will never ever cease.

So don't think that Nonny's love is gone
      Or that her life is through,
For God has many special things
      In mind for her to do.

And as Nonny lives on in Heaven,
      In whatever new life she finds,
She will be right here on earth with us
      In our hearts and in our minds.

And anyone who knew her
      Will feel the same today,
For love lives on forever
      If only in a brand new way.

A Close Friend

I have a friend, a very close friend

I think of him each time I pray.

He's my grandpa—I love him lots.

I wish to see him someday.

He died on February fifth, nineteen hundred,
   ninety-four.

I love my grandpa, he's the best,

His age was fifty-four.

I think of him each day

I miss you,

I wish you could have stayed.

by Erika Lynn Atherton
age 8
(my granddaughter)

Chapter Five

Loss Of Parents

Somehow I think we expect our parents will live forever. They were there for us as children and we fall into a false sense of security, making us feel as if they will always be there to praise our accomplishments or to pick up the pieces of our failures. Talk about an unconditional love! Our parents know everything (well, almost everything) bad we ever did in our lives from childhood to adulthood and they love us anyway. Losing their love and support through death is just as difficult for adult children as it is for young children.

As with any death, the losses reach out so much farther than the loss of a physical presence. With the death of our parents, we lose our position in the progression of life and are catapulted into the position of being the oldest generation. That can be frightening as well as an awesome responsibility. First of all, it awakens our awareness of our own mortality as we become "next in line," so to speak. Being the oldest generation is the last stage of family progression. Secondly, if we looked to our parents for advice or wisdom, that source of knowledge is no longer available. All of a sudden, we acquire the status of the all-knowing head of the family and our children and grandchildren come to us for the same answers we sought from our parents. How do we make the transition? Have we learned enough from our parents to pass along to future generations? If the parents are still young when they die, the answer is probably "no," but if we are adults, the answer must be "yes" as new generations have been tapping into the wisdom of the oldest generation for centuries. However, as my mother, who was my veritable gold-mine of information, slipped away with Alzheimer's and my father was already dead, I felt unqualified to assume her knowledgeable role. There were many answers to so many unasked questions that died with them both.

With the death of my husband, one of my greatest laments related to the same unfortunate situation. I kept saying over and over, "The children are not ready to lose their father. They still had so much to learn from him. What will they ever do?" The answer seems to be that when you lose your father and his practical knowledge, you resort to learning by trial and error or even by seeking the advice of others. We learn a lot from our mistakes, even more than from our successes. I suffice to say that my children have learned a lot since their father died!

My children were very close to their father, especially my daughter. She was the apple of his eye and, according to him, she never did anything wrong. I might tell a slightly different story, but she was "Daddy's little girl" and he spoiled her rotten. She was in her late teens when he died, and she proceeded to fulfill the text book profile of a girl who loses her father when she is a teenager. She became restless and undecided, changing her major in college studies several times, transferring to different colleges, and changing her life altogether. Her first change was to move out of the college dorm where she could no longer tolerate the giddiness of the girls when she was in such pain. As no one goes through grief and remains the same, my daughter matured beyond her years.

After her third college and fourth major, then dropping out of school entirely, she added to the classic profile by falling in love with and marrying a man who was several years her senior. But then, who could blame her? I say this with absolutely no prejudice at all, but there is very little not to love about my son-in-law. Whether it was a coincidence or whether my daughter fell into an established category of grieving teenage girls is unimportant. The important thing is that she found love, happiness, and healing.

My two sons were both married with children of their own when their father died. Both of their lives changed completely after his death. Who would think that one death could create so many life-altering situations. My oldest son was with his father when he died suddenly of a heart attack. They were the last two riders in a group of snowmobilers just heading out for a day's ride. As my husband's machine just went more and more slowly, he slid off and came to rest in the snow. Rushing to his side, my son tried to

68

revive him, waiting for the others to look back and return to help in what seemed like an eternity instead of moments. For me, it was comforting to know my son was with him, that he did not die alone. For my son, it added to his grief as it raised many questions. "What more could I have done? If I had done something different would he still be alive?" These were two of the most haunting ones. What a burden to put upon himself. But it is typical in all deaths to feel some measure of guilt for whatever reason and it is difficult to let go of it.

When the other snowmobilers returned, someone else administered CPR until the ambulance arrived to no avail, and I am sure nothing my son could have done would have made a difference. However, he will always carry one memory that the rest of the family does not have, seeing his father look up at him, hyperventilating, and then closing his eyes forever. My last memory of him is one of laughter as he joked on his way out the door that morning. Oh, how I wish I could trade memories with my son to help ease his pain.

To add to my son's grief and turmoil, he lost more than just his father, he lost his financial security. He worked for his father in a business which was jointly owned with a partner. In the partnership agreement, my husband's share of the business went to his partner, not to my son or myself. It was very difficult for my son to go to work every day, passing by his father's empty office. It became even harder when someone new took over the office and sat behind the desk. He went from being an owner's son to just another employee and was soon handed a demotion which started only after he trained his replacement.

I have a great admiration for my son, as most men would have walked out with such treatment, but his family came first. He could not afford to leave without another means of support, and he endured his grief and humiliation until the right opportunity presented itself. I also have a great admiration for my daughter-in-law who was very supportive and understanding of my son's grief over both losses. People do not always realize how important their support is for those who are grieving. Though they cannot do the grieving for us, their support is a much needed and beneficial part of the healing process for grief. Lack of understanding only adds to the pain.

My youngest son lived a thousand miles away and therefore his father was not a part of his daily life. Although not having one's daily life affected is helpful in the total grieving process as constant reminders are not presenting themselves as often, being so far away offers its own variety of regrets and pain. For my son there were many regrets not seeing his father in almost a year, his children would never know their grandfather, guilt at living too far away to be of help to me, and the list goes on.

A year after his father died, my son was diagnosed with diabetes. With neither my husband or I nor either of our parents having diabetes, I cannot help but wonder if its onset had anything to do with his grief for his father. In his book, *Understanding Grief*, Edgar Jackson states that research shows many physical diseases and ailments can be traced to unresolved grief with a specific reference to diabetes. Grief affects more than our emotional and mental state, it also affects our physical body. As no tests were taken at its point of discovery to determine why he had diabetes with the only concern being that he had the disease, my son will probably never know how he ended up with insulin shots twice a day.

With his grief for his father and this seemingly devastating news, my son panicked, convincing himself that he, too, would die young. In rushing to achieve all his lifetime goals in the short span he envisioned as his time left on earth, he made several hasty decisions which cost him dearly, both financially and emotionally. But through it all, he found a faith strong enough to see him through, provide him with a grounding to what is really important in life, and return him to his original career. And once again, my praise goes to his wife who supported him through it all. Although we were only a phone call away, she was his only "hands-on" support group while the rest of us had a wide circle of close family nearby.

All the children have worked their way through their grief, putting it into perspective as their lives have changed for the better. It took time, patience, love, and faith, but they are all survivors. They are all closer as siblings as they were drawn together to

70

provide the strength for one another that was once provided by their father. Siblings can go both ways after losing a parent. They can become closer, or they can move away from each other. The first six months, when emotions were running high for all of us and fuses were short, I wondered if we would ever be a family again. But as the children began to heal, they moved into closer relationships as they discovered through their loss that love and family is what life is all about.

My children were young adults when their father died, but younger children also grieve the loss of their parents and need time to mourn. According to Helen Fitzgerald who wrote *The Grieving Child* as well as *The Mourning Handbook,* a young child may feel abandoned by the parent who dies and could perhaps transfer that feeling to all relationships later in life, unconsciously feeling that everyone will leave him or her. Children also may not understand the full finality of death, still wanting to see and be with their dead parent. Helping children of all ages to express their grief through tears, spoken or written words, through arts and crafts, or by some method of counseling to release their deep emotions will provide the foundation for healing. Another positive healing tool is to involve them in the funeral rites and rituals either actively or with basic information.

When my father died, I was in my early thirties. There is a common belief suggesting that daughters are often closer to their fathers, while sons are closer to their mothers. This is not always true. I did not share that special relationship with my father. For the most part, Dad was just there, never involving himself in my life unless he thought I needed to hear one of his never-ending lectures and not having much patience with his own children. His patience was reserved for his students. There was one month a year that his guard came down (I would say he let his hair down, but he did not have that much hair to let down). For the whole month of July every year while I was growing up, we camped on Lake Champlain. Those were the days of my fondest memories of my father. Since he had no sons, he taught my sister and me how to fish, how to gather the frogs he used for bait, and how to bait our own hooks. Unfortunately, he also taught us to clean the fish (at least the perch; fileting bass was something he saved for himself), a fact that I never revealed to my ice-fishing husband who would bring home several hundred perch at a time.

Dad's attitude and personality changed during July, not just with the fishing but in other ways as well. He spent time with us and enjoyed being with us. The other eleven months I was basically embarrassed by his attitude with my friends and even more embarrassed that his students knew of his drinking problem. He was not a falling-down-drunk abusive alcoholic. He just *needed* to drink and tried to hide his drinking by hiding his liquor. He started drinking when his own father died, burdened with grief he could not or would not express any other way.

By the time I was married and had my first two children, my father and I finally came to understand each other and actually enjoy each other. Not that the past was erased, but a new father-daughter relationship emerged and I reveled in having the father I had wanted in my childhood. However, our new relationship was cut short by his sudden death, just two years after it began. For a long time I felt cheated out of having a father once again, but I finally reached a point where I felt fortunate to have re-discovered my father as an adult, through adult eyes and understanding, and to see him change as he had finally stopped drinking.

My grief for my father was not on the same level as my daughter's grief had been for her father. I grieved for a lost relationship, but to say I mourned the loss of his person would be hypocritical. He harbored so many fears that he had, in a sense, given up living, withdrawing away from friends and social contacts, retreating to the security of his home and family, sitting for hours on end in front of a television as real life was passing him by. I just could not wish him back — at least not for me. I did feel my mother's pain, however, and I grieved for her loss more than my own. My new relationship with my father was not a strong bond of love, but more of an acceptance of who he was, both as a person and as my father.

I felt guilty for my feelings, or lack of them I guess you might say, but my guilt did not last long or prevent me from healing. What lasted for years was my feeling that I had disappointed him for not finishing college and for not doing something more profound with my life. He'd had such high hopes for me and being a cosmetologist was not one of them. Perhaps I disappointed myself as well, not that I would have changed my life as it was and is because of the choices I made, but because I had graduated as valedictorian of my class, was voted most likely to succeed, and I felt a certain obligation to those honors. My success, however, is relevant only to one's definition of success, and I think on some level, my father actually came to fit his definition of success into my life's accomplishments even though they were not on his academic ideal level of success. But the world still equates success with fame and fortune which definitely does not define my success in life.

I think the shock of the suddenness of my father's death played the biggest part in my emotional reaction. A sudden unexpected death leaves family and friends reeling from disbelief, which in itself is difficult to cope with and makes the grief more difficult. There was never a chance to say good-bye to my father, or to say those last few things I needed to say to "clear the air," so to speak. But, as with my step-grandmother, I worked through those unfinished regrets by writing, talking, and praying.

While my relationship with my father was somewhat strained, my relationship with my mother was one of adoration. I adored her and loved her for all her endearing qualities. To me, she was an angel. She was soft-spoken, rarely raising her voice, and certainly never uttering any profanity either aloud or to herself. I remember once when our gas stove lashed out at her with a small burst of flames from her attempt to ignite it, my sister and I thought for a brief moment that this would be the one time we would hear our mother say some terrible word. However, as she seemed to be working herself up to a point of no return, she finally softly said, "Oh, darn!" What a disappointment for two teenage girls! Actually, that is one of the qualities I admired about her. I am afraid that I cannot claim the same restraint with my frustrations.

My mother taught us to sew, knit, crochet (the crocheting was limited to me as my sister was left-handed and my mother, try as she might, could not seem to transfer the stitches into a left-handed direction), and to play cards and games with never-ending patience.

73

She was active in the community, her church, and she was the assistant treasurer at a local bank. She was everything I wanted to be, except in her relationship with my father. There she was submissive to his controlling nature, the one quality I could not bring myself to agree with or admire, although I did admire her commitment to her marriage.

I also admired her for her knowledge (she was valedictorian of both her high school and college graduating class) and I loved her for who she was. The night before my wedding, I curled up in her lap for one last embrace as her "little girl" and we talked way into the night. From that moment on, she always treated me as a capable adult, never offering unsolicited advice, never interfering with my marriage or child-rearing, and always showering me with praise for my abilities, whether it was for cooking, raising the children, doing hairstyles, writing poetry, or fashioning handwork. She never realized that the more she patted me on the back, the more she praised herself, as it was from her example that I learned how to balance my life's activities, how to emanate my love, how to live.

Her death came three times for me: when her personality changed due to her Alzheimer's Disease, when she no longer remembered anything or anyone, and when her physical body died. And I lost two people when she died. I lost the mother I knew, and the person she had become in her dementia, the one I had become as emotionally attached to as much as I loved who she had been. I began the grief process before she even died. As she moved through the stages of her illness, I moved through many aspects and emotions of grief, distancing myself by accepting her fate. But even with much time for preparation, nothing really prepares you for the finality that comes with death. It is still a shock, it is still painful, and it still needs time for healing.

My mother's death put me in the oldest generation status and left me, in effect, orphaned. As ready as I thought I was to have her vegetative life come to an end, I suddenly felt alone. Somewhere along the way we had reversed roles. She needed me as a small child needs its mother and not being needed anymore only added to my loneliness. That, and the fact that I had become emotionally attached to the child-like person my mother had become through her dementia. Visiting her at the nursing home was part of my routine and to have it end abruptly left me feeling empty and lost.

I remember thinking years ago that visiting a funeral home for calling hours was a barbaric thing to do. Standing beside a casket with a dead loved one inside was not something I thought I could ever do. I saw it as just a money-making ritual for funeral homes. My disgust was heightened when someone would pass by the casket and then comment on how good the person looked. How could one look good when he or she was dead? Well, my mother looked good. To this day, I wish I had taken a picture. She no longer had sunken eyes, the look of anguish, or that blank stare I had come to know so well. She looked like the mother I had almost forgotten, resting peacefully as if she were sleeping. I would not have missed that last look at my mother for anything. For that brief moment, I was transported in time to happier days when I sat in my mother's lap and looked to her for reassurance, comfort, and love. And I found it once again.

I think it is difficult to lose a mother under any circumstance. Allowing for the fact that there are always exceptions to every rule, I think there is a deeper sense of loss when our mothers die than when our fathers do. I am not just making an assumption because I was closer to my mother than I was to my father, but because mothers have such a predominant role in our birth that continues throughout our lives. There is a bond between mother and child that begins long before a father has any role to fulfill. Mothers are co-creators with God and we, as children, are apt to see them as part divine, as prime examples to follow. This bond makes the journey through grief over their death a very sorrowful and painful one.

For me, my mother's death was a painful prelude for an even more traumatic death. There are times when I think her death prepared me for my husband's death and often thought I never could have survived his death if I had not gained so much spiritual strength from hers. Yet there are also times when I grieved more for her after my husband died than before. When we are sick or hurt, we want our mothers. They seem to make us feel better, just by being there, and they always know just what to do or say. Well, that is what I wanted after my husband died. I wanted my mother to make it all better, to make the pain go away. I needed her and she was not there. I would have given anything just to curl up on her lap with her soft voice soothing my heartache. So, I missed her even more and as I grieved for my husband, I grieved for her.

Like becoming a teenager, turning twenty-one, and turning fifty, death is a point of time reference, determining when both preceding and post-death experiences happen and a parent's death is often the one that becomes our time line. It is not a conscious decision to mark time with the event of death, it just happens. There was not much time after my mother's death to relate happenings without overlapping with my husband's death. Since his death was more traumatic and more recent, I tend to relate events to either before he died or after he died. Sometimes, however, I combine the two into one time-line and say something happened before my mother died or after my husband died. I especially place events such as births and weddings of friends and family in a before and after time-line. For instance, I would say that my sons were married before my mother died but my daughter was married after my husband died. When I am asked to come up with a date for an event that I do not specifically remember, I always start at one death or the other and count backward or forward to try and jog my memory as to the exact date.

Whether we expect our parents to die due to illness or age, or whether we lose them suddenly, the death of a parent brings forth many emotions. It changes our perspective as we begin to look at life through the eyes of the older generation. It changes our life pattern of having someone to turn to when we need love, praise, comfort, advice, or even financial assistance. It is a devastating loss to most of us. And for those who do not mourn the passing of a parent due to strained relationships, the loss harbors unresolved feelings and regrets. Either way, losing a parent changes our lives.

Oh, So Softly

Softly, oh so softly,
    My mother spoke to me.
She never raised her voice at all
    She never crossed me on her knee.

Softly, oh so softly,
    My mother guided me along.
She taught me when to be gentle
    And when I should be strong.

Softly, oh so softly,
    She influenced my life.
She taught me through her quiet strength
    How to deal with daily strife.

Softly, oh so softly,
    Just as gentle as a lamb,
She taught me all the things I'd need
    To make me who I am.

Softly, oh so softly
    My mother gave to me,
A love to last a lifetime
    And through all eternity.

Softly, oh so softly,
    My mother lost all knowing.
But even then, everyone could see
    Her great gentleness still showing.

Her gentle ways and gone now,
    For she has left this world she trod,
But I can still feel her love with me
    As she now softly walks with God.

Your Own Special Angel

Your mother was so special
        Not just to all of you;
For myself and many others
        Felt the warmth of her love, too.

Her heart welcomed in so many
        For it was like an open door.
She kept us all deep inside
        And there was always room for more.

She was always there to listen,
        And shared our troubles one by one;
And after helping us through bad times
        She rejoiced in all our fun.

Life will not be the same without her
        Now that she has gone away,
But in your heart and in your mind
        She will be with you every day.

For, your mother will never leave you
        If you carry her inside.
The memories that belong to you
        Will live long after your tears have dried.

So, do not shed wild tears for her,
        Just cry for your family.
It is always sad to say "good-bye"
        And they will miss her company.

From her new home she will send you
        All her love both night and day.
She is now your own special angel
        To help guide you along your way.

Mother

An angel on earth, you were always there
To help us through each and every care.
You gave us your guidance through the years.
You embraced our joys, and wiped our tears.
You carried your heartaches deep within;
Always lifting our spirits with your loving grin.
Then, one day we reversed roles with you
And the power of your love saw us all through.
The deep bond of your love was truly God-given;
First an angel on earth, and now one in heaven.

Our Hearts Remember

Our hearts remember
　　　　how you calmed our fears.
　　　　You soothed our pain
　　　　and dried our tears.

You gave us guidance
　　　　with your gentle touch.
　　　　You gave us praise,
　　　　and loved us much.

Our hearts are warm
　　　　when we think of you.
　　　　We feel your love
　　　　in all we do.

Miracles For Your Father

There are so many miracles
That happen every day:
Rainbowed skies,
Newborn cries,
And sunshine to light our way.

The changing of the seasons,
The perfection of the rose,
Moonlit walks,
Quiet talks,
And the way the river flows.

If you can see these miracles
That unfold before your eyes,
Then you know,
For they all show
That no one ever truly dies.

For the miracles of nature
And those of heart and mind,
Depict a role,
For the soul
That follow laws of another kind.

There is no death in nature,
Just a continuing rebirth.
It is true,
For humans, too,
Born anew after life on earth.

Your father is no exception
To the law of immortality.
He is not gone,
His soul lives on
In heaven and in your memory.

His life was not one lived in vain,
        He had a purpose to fulfill.
        Work to do,
        Family, too
As he carried out God's Will.

And now God's Will has taken him
        To a place you cannot see.
        But his essence,
        And his presence
Are here with you and will always be.

If Only

"If" is such a big question
　　　For being a tiny word,
And often when you ask "Why?"
　　　The question goes unanswered.

If only you knew why your mother
　　　Had to be taken from this earth.
If only you knew if her death
　　　Had any meaning or any worth.

If only her life had been longer
　　　And had not ended with such sorrow.
If only she could be here
　　　To help you through each tomorrow.

How many times did you say, "If"?
　　　How many times did you ask, "Why?"
And the question asked most often,
　　　"Why did my mother die?"

You may think there is no answer
　　　To these questions in your mind,
But if you listen with your heart
　　　The answer you will find.

The answer will not come easy —
　　　You have to believe in God's Love,
And trust He needed your mother
　　　To be with Him in heaven above.

And though her life here has ended,
　　　Her love will always shine through.
She will give you strength and courage
　　　In everything you do.

And if you don't believe me,
    Just close your eyes real tight,
And hear your biggest fan of all
    Cheering you on both day and night.

Fear No More, My Dad

My father left so suddenly
    I could not say good-bye,
And deep inside, it hurt so bad
    That all I could do was cry.

I cried for my dear mother
    Whom Dad had left behind,
And wondered if she'd be alright
    In her heart and in her mind.

Then I cried for my dear sister
    And the pain that she must feel;
Then I cried for my own self,
    With all my heart to reveal.

But, I could not cry for you, Dad,
    Because I believe with all my heart
That you are living with God now
    Although still with us in part.

I know God's love has touched you
    And your new life has begun;
Living a life of love and peace
    As warm as the summer sun.

And when I close my eyes real tight,
    I can see your face aglow;
For, the fear you've always lived with,
    Now, wondrously doesn't show.

And now you know the secret
    Of the faith Mother always had,
And why I say with all my love. . .
    Fear no more, my Dad.

In Remembrance

Your mother will be remembered
  By those of us who care.
Her family, friends, and neighbors
  Have many memories to share.

Her life has touched so many
  In a way no one can measure.
Her time and work with children
  Is a memory so many treasure.

And though the last years of her life
  Brought her troubles by the score,
She'll live on within all our hearts
  As we remember her from before.

We never will know exactly why
  Your mother had to suffer so.
Only God has all the answers
  And there is no need for us to know.

For faith tells us when this life ends,
  All our troubles are meaningless,
For in our new life lived with God,
  We will be filled with happiness.

Your mother knew she would find that joy
  Filled with everlasting peace,
And the love that now surrounds her
  Will never ever cease.

Yes, your mother is at peace now,
  In a peace she has never known.
Her faith knew it existed,
  But now she has it for her own.

And knowing she is at peace with God
　　Will soon bring you peace, too.
And though her home is now in heaven,
　　Her love will be here with you.

A Mother's Love Lives On

There is no love that is greater
Than that of a mother's love.
It is filled with warmth and goodness,
For it comes from heaven above.

God made the love so special
So that we would always know
The power of His own love
In a way that it would show.

He made mothers in His likeness
To be creators here on earth,
And just like Him, they always live;
Their death is just a rebirth.

I can hear the angels singing
As heaven's gates are opened wide,
As God gently embraces your mother
And then places her at His side.

So, wipe away your tears now,
And know your mother is living still,
In a new life of truth and beauty,
Of perfect peace and goodwill.

No more earthly pain or troubles;
They have all been washed away.
There is such joy and happiness
And complete love to fill each day.

And, as your mother's love lives on,
It will always be with you,
To give you strength and courage
In everything you do.

For, the bond has not been broken;
Your mother's love is much too strong.
She will send her love from heaven
Every day, your whole life long.

And even as a mother's love
Is a bond that never ends,
I pray you will find comfort
In the bond that makes us friends.

And may you also find solace
Knowing your mother is not alone,
In knowing she is reunited
With your father in their new home.

I'll Never Forget

I'll never forget the last time he came
      And drank a glass of wine.
He said he was a little shaky
      But would be fine in a short time.

He told me it would be springtime
      Before he was himself again,
But I thought by the twinkle in his eye
      That it might be before then.

I'll never forget how he played the drums
      And shot the game of pool,
Nor the gleam in his eye when he said,
      "You know, I used to play this in school."

Though he did not stay very long that day,
      The memory will never dim;
And will always be one of my favorites
      Every time I think of him.

Memories

Memories are so precious
    When someone says, "good-bye."
Memories keep within our hearts
    A love that can never die.

And memories of your mother
    Will last your whole life long.
Because she was so special,
    The memories will stay strong.

Her love for her family
    Was as deep as it could be;
Every member was important to her,
    That was very plain to see.

Her love did not stop with family ties
    And for one reason or another,
There were many young men and women
    Who, with love, all called her "Mother."

Her life and love touched so many
    That everywhere you go,
Someone will share a memory
    Of a story you may not know.

It could be one of a dinner
    That she used to cater with ease.
No matter what the menu,
    It was always sure to please.

And then there are those golfers
    Who will remember all the fun
Of playing cards with your mother
    After the matches were all done.

She opened up her heart and home
　　　To countless Norwich boys.
The memories of her helping hand
　　　Still bring them many joys.

Your mother and the Red Mitten
　　　Are almost one in the same;
Her beautiful crafts and handwork
　　　Will be a lasting tribute to her name.

I pray God will bring you comfort
　　　Through these memories that are so dear
And in knowing she is in heaven
　　　But her spirit will always be near.

And if you still need more comfort,
　　　Then feel the love I send:
— Because she was your mother
　　　— Because she was my friend.

Chapter Six

The Death Of A Child

One of life's greatest sorrows is the death of a child, and many who have lost a child would probably say it is the worst grief to bear. It goes against the natural order of life where the oldest are expected to die first. When an older person dies, one of the first comments we hear is, "At least he or she had a good life." We tend to measure a "good life" by its longevity rather than by quality, so when a child dies, we mourn not only the loss of the life that was, but also the life that will never be fulfilled.

The regrets associated with losing a child are numerous and often go beyond reason. The regret that a child died before its parents, leads the parents to feel guilty for still being alive. A parent assumes the role of protector with the birth of a child, and his or her early death is then seen as a failure — failure to protect that child from harm, failure to be able to change places with him or her in order to save its life.

We think of children as being a part of their parents, created by them to be half of the mother, half of the father. It is easy to see why death leaves parents with the feeling that part of them died too — the part of themselves they gave to their child is gone, creating a void where they once created life.

But there is more. Helen Fitzgerald, a certified death educator, explains in her book, *The Mourning Handbook,* that with the loss of a child, you not only lose part of your future but also part of your immortality. Your future is affected because you lose all the experiences you would have shared with your child, including grandchildren to treasure. And as we gain a measure of immortality from our grandchildren and great-grandchildren, Fitzgerald cites this as another loss to mourn.

Grieving for a child has to be one of the most extreme pressures that a marriage has to endure. When you lose your mother, it is *your* mother. She is a mother-in-law to your spouse. No one expects the emotions of grief to be exactly the same. It is true for other losses as well, such as fathers, friends, and grandparents. And if you lose your spouse, you are the only spouse left to grieve. Everyone around you is grieving for a slightly different relationship in all deaths except that of two parents grieving for their child as they share the same loss. The individual aspects of grief which cause our external expressions to be different are not as great a factor when relationships to the deceased are varied. However, when a child dies, both parents share the same loss, the same relationship. From personal experience, I know that sharing grief is at best difficult, if not impossible. Parents who can share their grief are very fortunate and will undoubtedly draw closer together than ever. But what if they cannot help each other grieve? If one parent grieves silently, the parent who is grieving outwardly may not understand that silent grief is as intense as crying profusely, it is just not as visible.

In addition to different expressions of their grief, parents may place the blame for the child's death on their spouse, creating more conflict. This blame may be completely unfounded, but it is part of grief. When my husband died, I blamed his partner's unsettled personal life as being the catalyst for his heart attack, I blamed the doctor in the emergency room for not doing enough to revive him, and I blamed myself. If spouses turn their blame toward each other, the heartache would be devastating, sometimes too devastating to heal even when their grief begins to heal. If there are other children in the family, the difference in the way parents react to them may also be a source of conflict. One parent might turn to the other children while the spouse puts the dead child on a pedestal that the other children can never reach. There are so many differences that can lead to stress in a marriage after the loss of a child.

Fortunately, I have never experienced the death of a child, but many of my friends and family have suffered this great sorrow. I have seen grief separate as well as strengthen a couple's relationship, and some have found their way back to each other only after their grief began to heal. When you are grieving, you do not always think rationally. If your spouse does not express his or her emotions the way you do, it is easy to feel your grief is greater, becoming angry that your spouse must not care as much as you do. I have seen one mother whose grief was uncontrollably expressed with constant tears consider her husband's quiet withdrawn reaction as a personal insult to their dead child. If he had been grieving for another family member other than a child, his demeanor would have been considered a tribute to his faith and to the deceased loved one.

It is one thing for friends and family to judge our grief wrongly, to offer advice on what is their view of the "proper" way to grieve, but when spouses cannot reach out and understand each other's grief, it can add to the pain and anger which is already included in the grief process. I would think that open communication between grieving spouses is very important for their relationship to survive intact.

Another point to consider is the prevalent belief that we never come through grief as the same person we were before the death. If husband and wife both emerge from unshared grief as different people, they may no longer share the same goals and ideals, likes and dislikes, love and mutual respect. Marriages that do survive a child's death are a testament to understanding and love.

It was the death of a child that began shaping my life into who I am today. Although there have been many events and subsequent deaths that have had a great impact on the changes in my life, the death of a nine-year-old girl who died from Rye's Syndrome laid the foundation for my journey into writing poetry which eventually led me back to acquiring a college degree in Religion through a writing and arts program.

I had never written a poem before her death except in high school English class. I did not make a conscious decision to write a poem, it just sort of happened. When the telephone call came asking my husband to be the pall bearer, I did all the things one does when someone dies. I cooked and baked, ordered flowers, visited the parents, and bought a beautiful sympathy card. But I could not just sign my name. We were too close to the parents and I needed to add a personal message. But what does one say to someone who has just lost a child? Well, as a young 25 year old mother myself, I surely did not know. Nothing sounded right until I finally put my thoughts into a poem which came as if someone were dictating the words to me after I pleaded for divine inspiration. Since then, I have written many poems of comfort for friends and family and for my own healing. Writing is therapeutic and creating poems helped heal my own grief as much as, if not more than, they comforted anyone else.

The first of my poems to be read at a funeral was also written as the result of the death of a child, a sixteen-year-old boy who not only would never do normal boyish things in the future, he could not do them throughout his life as he was confined to a wheelchair with Muscular Dystrophy. It is difficult to think of what he missed without remembering what he gave to everyone around him. As I listened to my poem being read, I was filled with as much emotion as when I wrote it, bringing tears to my eyes. This ability to illicit emotions and bring them to the surface is one of the therapeutic values of poetry, of all writing.

As with any death, the final comfort in the loss of a child is the memories of his or her life. The physical body is gone, the future experiences are gone, but even death cannot destroy the memories. Through our memories, children remain forever young and forever loved, even as they are forever mourned. To go forward after a child's death is to give meaning to that death and to his or her life. And there is meaning in all lives, no matter how young the child is, no matter the cause of death. Finding the meaning encompassed in the short lifetime and in the tragedy of death is finding hope, a reason to live again in spite of the loss.

Free At Last

Sometimes it doesn't seem quite fair
The way life turns out for some.
We stop and wonder why we are here
And from where we could have come.

But after all the questions cease
And the pain begins to fade,
Our hearts and minds tell us so true
It is by God that we were made.

And though Paul's life with you seemed short
And filled with too much pain,
Remember that by God's eternal time
He will live a long tomorrow.

For now he is free to run and jump
And play with all God's children,
And free from yesterday's earthly body
That limited him so back then.

And though Paul's earthly body
Seemed to fail him while he was here,
His soul was strengthened and nourished
By your love, which he held dear.

A love which was returned to you
A thousand fold or more,
A bond that will remain with you
Until you and Paul meet at God's door.

Till then, I know you would find comfort,
And find it, oh, so fast,
If you could just hear Paul saying,
"Don't cry — I'm free at last."

Springtime

It is Springtime in the Heavens,
    Of this, I am quite certain,
For God has added one more flower
    To His perfect holy garden.

He chose a very special one,
    Young and beautiful and strong
To give Heaven new life and laughter,
    To give His choir a brand new song.

And just as a fresh Spring breeze
    That warms the month of May,
Your daughter's love continues on
    Filling your heart with warmth each day.

Her smile will be a memory
    For you to always cherish.
Her laughter planted in your mind
    Will surely not ever perish.

She will blossom in her goodness
    Fulfilling an eternal plan,
Rising to new heights of joy
    Far beyond where she began.

So, as the balmy breezes blow
    And the rain mixes with your tears,
The new glory in the sunshine
    Will warm your heart for many years.

The promise of each Springtime
    As life renews beneath the snow
Assures us all that life goes on
    In ways we do not know.

So, though you cannot see or touch
  Your daughter's new living form
You will feel her love flow through you
  Even above the raging storm.

And when the gardens start to bloom
  And Springtime is in the air,
In all you see around you,
  You will feel your daughter there.

Our Prayer

Dear Father, Who art in heaven,
  We come to you in prayer.
We ask for your love and comfort
  To heal the sorrow that we bear.

We need your strength and courage
  To help us through each day.
We need to feel a peace within
  To help take our pain away.

Is this the pain you bore alone
  When you watched your own son die?
How did you keep this world turning
  When it would have been easier just to cry?

It is hard for us to understand
  The depth of the love you shared,
Feeling sadness and sorrow for Jesus
  Just to show how much you cared.

Your pain was washed away quickly
  On that glorious Easter day.
And once again you showed your love
  As you took Jesus to Heaven to stay.

And now, you are taking our son
  To live with you in Heaven above.
Please let him share in your Glory
  And embrace him with your love.

Even through our pain and our tears
  And our grief that has no measure,
We thank you for his life with us.
  He was a gift we will always treasure.

In our hearts, he will live forever.
In our minds, memories will never cease.
Father, we pray as this world must keep turning,
Please turn our pain into joy and peace.

Forever in Your Heart

To lose a son such as yours
      Must seem too unreal to accept.
And the nightmare must get stronger
      With each tear you have wept.

I wish I could ease the pain you feel
      And wash away your tears,
But I know your great sorrow
      Will only ease through the years.

Words somehow seem empty
      As you struggle to say, "Good-bye,"
Leaving you with many questions
      As you ask yourselves, "Why?"

How could God have needed him
      More than you as parents would?
What special plan did your son fill
      That no one else ever could?

Perhaps your questions will remain
      Unanswered while you are on earth,
But one day when you reach life's end,
      You will clearly see your son's worth.

For life and death have a purpose,
      And though we may question His ways,
God holds each life as precious,
      No matter for how many days.

I believe this very strongly
      That God is a certainty,
And that your son is with Him now
      Throughout all eternity.

It may seem as if he is far away,
      Out of your reach and your sight,
But his spirit is very close at hand
      As you remember him day and night.

And as each memory comes to you,
      The more you will realize
That your son is very much alive
      Though not in a form visible to your eyes.

For he will live forever in your heart,
      In a place made by your love.
A love that he still shares with you
      From his place with God above.

We'll Be Seeing You Again

Through our tears we remember you
    With that twinkle in your eye,
And how at times you seemed to be
    Just a little bit too shy.

And then there were those baseball years
    That gave you so much pleasure,
The snowmobile that you rode and rode
    Over miles no one could measure.

You will live on forever
    Within our hearts and our minds.
As we lovingly remember you
    And your antics of all kinds.

We know that you will be there
    When we reach God's Golden Door,
Keeping the Heaven's lively
    Until we are with you once more.

So, knowing you are now with God,
    Yet still with us now and then,
Instead of saying sad goodbyes,
    "We'll be seeing you again."

Why Leanne?

One special day a few years ago,
    A baby boy was born.
God gave him a soul like yours and mine
    Though Nature did not adorn.

So, God decided then and there
    To give the family His love,
To help them through the time they had
    Until Joe was taken above.

But one thing God did not know
    That on top of the love He gave,
The family there already shared
    A love on which He could rave.

And now, the time was drawing near,
    But what was God to do?
He couldn't take Joe 'till he could provide
    All the love he'd grown used to.

So, He looked to His saints and angels,
    Then searched the wide world o'er,
But none could match the love so rare
    given behind the Lafreniere door.

God thought and thought and thought some more
    Of all the things he could do,
And then He knew even with all His love,
    He needed Leanne's, too.

Then He took Leanne to live with Him
    And showed her what to do,
So she could take the same care of Joe
    As when he was with you.

Now, if you don't believe me,
      Just close your eyes real tight,
And see Leanne and Joey
      Walking together in God's Light.

And when you all get to Heaven
      You'll wonder at this no more,
For Leanne and Joey will be right there
      To greet you at the door.

Chapter Seven

Death Of A Friend Or Sibling

The first conscious memory of my life concerns the eventual death of a friend. Actually, he was probably my only friend at the time as we were both just two years old. Born on the same day and living in a duplex shared by our parents, my friend and I must have spent a lot of time together in those first two years. But my little friend was stricken with leukemia and soon he was too weak to play with me. That is my first recollection — me, standing at his crib, looking through the slats, crying because he could not (I am sure I thought he *would not*) play with me.

As far as his death itself, I do not have any clear memory. I am sure I did not go to the funeral, but I often wonder what my parents said to me, if they said anything at all. Perhaps they thought I was too young to be told anything about death. From my vantage point of today, I wonder why I never asked my parents how they handled the questions I must have asked about where my little friend was. Looking back, I know that I did not understand the nature of grief until after my parents died, leaving no one to ask. I can assume, however, since two-year-olds were still considered babies when I was young, and parents were not as open with children as they are today, that mine probably did not see a need to discuss my loss as they tended to the needs of their friends who had just lost a son.

It is impossible to shelter children from exposure to death as death is as much a part of life as living. It is all around us. Death cannot be ignored and grief should not be ignored either, even for a child. Whatever awareness the age of the child allows should be addressed. When my husband died, my daughter-in-law very compassionately let her children make their own decision as to how involved they wanted to be in all the family gatherings and activities which took place during the first few days. Just as with adults, what was right for one child was not what the other one needed to deal with the death of their grandfather. The children were five, eight, and nine years old at the time and made their decisions based on their individual personalities rather than having their ages be the major factor. They were neither forced to take part in anything that might add to their grief nor were they denied participation in any of the events in which they wanted to be included. There was a great deal of communication between the adults and the children even if it was through many tears.

One day I was curled up on the couch, listening to a tape of hymns, with tears flowing as the grandchildren arrived. The obvious question posed was, "Why does Grammy listen to the music if it makes her cry?" The answer lies in the fact that both the music and the tears are healing, soothing and comforting. The children, who did not like seeing me sad, thought I was contributing to my sorrow by playing the tape. If I didn't cry, I would feel better. But crying is a release of emotion which eventually helps begin the healing process. It was a tough question to answer but my daughter-in-law explained it very well, and after hugs from them all, I dried my tears — for the moment.

As we get older and experience the loss of a friend through death, the emotional impact of grief goes very deep. There is no death that glaringly reminds us of our own fate more than the death of a friend. Many of our friends are near our own age, making us very aware that we could be next. As we grieve for our friend, we grieve for our own mortality.

There is a saying that we can choose our friends, but we cannot choose our relatives. Perhaps that is the major reason for the deep feelings of grief at their death as we chose that friend over anyone else because of who he or she was and how his or her personality complimented our own. The bond of love formed by friendship goes very deep, it goes to the soul. The emotional balance provided to us by our friendships shifts at death to leave an unbearable void. Statistics tell us that we only have one or two really close friends throughout our lifetime. Not that we do not have a circle of friends whom we enjoy; but true friendships based on love and trust are not around every corner, so if we lose one, that relationship is difficult, if not impossible, to replace.

Furthermore, we equate friends with happiness. We enjoy sharing things with them, doing things with them, and just being in their company. When a friend dies, one of our joys in life is taken away, replacing our happiness with extreme sorrow. Losing a part of our own happiness adds to the grief of losing the physical presence of our friend. With every death, we encounter a number of losses other than the actual death. Each death seems to spawn its own ripple effect as the person who died affected us in so many ways.

In today's transient society with job-related transfers or just seeking employment or a better pay scale, retirees moving to a warmer climate, adult children returning to care for aging parents, high school graduates going off to college or to serve in the military, death is not the only experience that produces a reaction of grief. When a close friend suddenly moves away for *any* reason, the separation can be as traumatic as an actual death, perpetuating all the emotions of grief.

The same is true for families who are separated by geography rather than death. Two of my children live almost a thousand miles away, and my step-daughter lives on the west coast of Canada, while I live in New England. The telephone is an often-used piece of equipment. Along with e-mail, the telephone bridges the gap in the distance for the adults, but not so with the young grandchildren. I am just a voice on the phone to the little ones. At the end of each visit, the separation brings a sense of loss — loss for all the stages and happenings in their lives that I will never see. And with that feeling of loss comes the emotion of grief. Perhaps for grandparents whose grandchildren all live a distance away, seeing them once or twice a year — or even less — is an accepted way of life. But for me, who has grandchildren close by so that I see the constant changes from their first smiles and steps to their first words and sentences, to their likes and dislikes, to their friends and first loves, to their sports and school concerts, and everything in between, having grandchildren who live far enough away to render that same relationship impossible emphasizes the reality of all the lost moments. It is for those lost moments that I grieve. Although it is true that the emotions and sense of loss I feel when I leave my grandchildren after a visit are minor compared to the emotions of grief after a death, they are nevertheless very real and are a part of my life's experiences.

Friendship of any kind, whether it is between family members or non-related friends, is a relationship we all value and cherish. When death or other forms of separation take that relationship away from us, we need to re-focus that part of our lives. As with any grief, we cannot rush through it after the loss of a friend, even if other people think we should. Some people do not understand that losing a friend can be more traumatic than losing a relative. But the truth is, we are often closer to friends than to relatives, and need a longer time to heal our grief after their death than others think we need from their judgmental assessment, thinking we should be beyond our grief when we are actually just beginning. Healing our emotions takes time and is a necessary part of learning to accept the death of a friend, and then to move beyond that loss.

The death of a sibling has the same impact on our realization that we also are mortal as does the death of a friend. There are other issues with siblings that are not associated with friends such as sibling rivalry, the differences in age and/or sex, our age when a sibling dies, the distance in miles between homes of adult children, whether or not the death of a sibling leaves us as the only child, and the closeness of the relationships. In recognizing that the relationships between siblings are the longest ongoing relationships in our lives, Nancy O'Connor, Ph.D. says, "There is often a profound feeling of sadness and sorrow, like losing some part of yourself. It is losing a part of your past, of common experiences and parents and places."

Since I have only one sister, I was never more thankful for her as when my mother was ill with Alzheimer's. Having someone to share the mental anguish, the added financial responsibilities, and all the decision-making duties made caring for my mother much easier than if I would have had to do it alone. I think my mother's illness is the one single issue that cemented my closeness with my sister as it put us in constant contact with each other in our otherwise busy scheduled lives. When a sibling dies, it often leaves just one or two children left to care for aging parents. I would not have wanted to be counted as the only surviving sibling, and can only imagine the grief, loneliness, and sole responsibilities created by such a loss.

Younger children experience feelings beyond those of adult siblings as they are often still feeling the competition of sibling rivalry. Helen Fitzgerald discusses this factor in her book, *The Mourning Handbook*, presenting the reality that a young surviving sibling may secretly feel glad that he or she no longer has to compete for parental attention or in any form of competition, for that matter. Fitzgerald also tells us this can create a strong feeling of guilt, especially if the surviving sibling is also glad to be the survivor. I do not think this pertains only to young siblings. A feeling of relief over the idea that someone else died instead of ourselves is a natural reaction at any age. I have experienced this feeling myself and admit it adds to the guilt associated with grieving. I would imagine the only relationships that might not produce feelings of relief to be the survivor would be a parent who loses a child or a child who loses a twin. The guilt comes from *being* the survivor, not in any sense of relief to be one.

Whether it be friends or a siblings, losing people close to us, and especially if close to our own age, is difficult to bear. We must find meaning and strength from the relationships and memories we shared, weaving them into who we are because we knew them and loved them.

For You, Bernie

For all the beautiful verses
        You sent on greeting cards,
For all the times we spent together
        On the golf course's many yards,
For the shower that you gave me
        With all our golfing friends,
For the friendship that you offered
        As a gift that never ends,
For all the laughter that we shared
        When life was going our way,
For all the moments we embraced
        When sadness ruled the day,
For the husband whom you gave your love,
        For the children whom you treasure,
For the grandchildren who filled your life
        With joy no one can measure,
For all the friends and family
        You helped along the way,
For all the cherished memories
        You leave with us today,
We thank God for your gift of life;
        We thank Him for your love,
And we send our love with you today
        To your new home in Heaven above.
For when our earthly bodies
        No longer need our soul,
It is love that remains between us
        To make our spirits whole.

A Lifetime Measured In Love

To have known her was to love her
Is the song so many sing,
For the moment anyone met her
She took them under her wing.

The wing was one of friendship
That came straight from her heart;
A feeling that you'd known her
Right from the very start.

For she had that way about her
That filled your life with glee;
Just to hear her lighthearted laughter
Would set a heavy heart free.

And now the wing that embraces
Is stronger than before,
For an angel's wings are greater
And hold love even more.

For all love comes from Heaven
Where she has gone to live,
But in our hearts and memories,
She still has much to give.

And though her life here seemed too short
And ended with too much pain,
Remember, a lifetime is measured in love
And not in the years we gain.

For some people you can know a lifetime
And never know them or their love,
But knowing Lola one day,
Was like knowing God above.

Memories Filled With Love

My house is full of memories
    Each one today is bringing tears;
But tomorrow they will bring a smile
    As I remember you through the years.

In one room, there are pictures
    Of my family that I treasure,
Sitting on a handmade shelf
    That you did so carefully measure.

A simple shelf that is painted white
    With scalloped braces for support,
Is now a cherished work of art
    With added beauty of a deeper sort.

In another room sits an angel
    Next to a granite clock.
They sit upon a shelving unit
    That you made solid as a rock.

In two rooms there are windows
    That are all both tall and wide;
Framed on top with wooden valences
    That stretch from side to side.

They add such charm and beauty
    To the windows that they grace,
And the curves on the scalloped edges
    Are all perfectly in place.

The toy room still includes a bed
    For Cabbage Patch-sized dolls.
The triple-decker bunks are used
    More often than bats and balls.

Even looking out my window,
        I can see some lattice work,
Designed and specially crafted
        To fulfill my latest quirk.

These physical reminders
        Though precious from the start,
Are not as deep and lasting
        As the memories of the heart.

I called you Clem Kadiddlehopper
        When your hair needed to be cut.
What a shame to have such wavy hair
        Wasted on such an ungrateful nut!

My name, in turn, was "Money Bags"
        Supposedly buried in my back yard;
Not only filled by cutting hair
        But also after a game with you of cards.

The card game was poker.
        How many memories they bring to mind!
When you would have a full house,
        Someone was sure to have four of a kind!

Sometimes the games got noisy
        If someone did not understand,
But even pitch games at the Mutuo
        Were loud after a real good hand.

My children loved to watch us play
        And you always treated them as your own;
Always there to make them smile and laugh
        Even after they were all grown.

And when they were grown with children,
    You extended your love even more,
And even held our Casey close to you
    The day her grandfather went through
    God's Door.

And now, you are passing through that Door,
    And there is one thing I must say,
I hope you and Glenn don't wear out the cards
    Before Elsie and I join you some day.

Until then, I know you will be happy
    In your new home up above,
As you will always be remembered here
    Through memories filled with love.

No Greater Love

There are so many different forms of love
That God has blessed us with from above.
There is, of course, His love for all the earth
From the tiny creatures that share their worth
With mankind, for whom His love is so great
That he sent his only Son to seal our fate;
To give us forgiveness for our every sin,
And to show us the way to live forever with Him.
There is the love shared between husband and wife,
A bond that grows deeper every day of their life.
That love seems stronger than any other
Until you witness the love of a mother.
The endless sacrifices that she makes
To give her children the guidance they will need
To follow life's path wherever it may lead.
The love between siblings can be very strong
As it endures competition and envy along
The way to a closeness that is only surpassed
By the deep-seated affection that is made to last.
A good teacher becomes great when there is love behind
The giving of knowledge to all the young minds.
The love in reverse is also heaven-sent:
Students' love for and teacher, a child's love for parents.
Friendship belongs on the top of love's lists,
For it is an integral part of each love that exists.
And a bond that is shared outside family ties
Is a love to be cherished through wondering eyes.
And there is no greater love between life-long friends
Than the love that is still there when the memory ends.
This made your mother special as she had in her heart
A unique loving quality to hold and to impart.
For this she will be remembered by the lives that she touched:
By her friends and her family whom she loved very much.

A New Start

Although your sister's short earthly life
    Was difficult to bear,
It was made much easier
    By knowing how much you care.

For there is a bond between sisters
    That blends the souls together;
A bond that strengthens through the years,
    A bond even death cannot sever.

And though her death came too soon
    And left you with a heavy heart,
Her difficulties have been wiped away
    As she is given a brand new start.

Her soul is free to soar above,
    To run through the heavenly streets,
And being reunited with your mother
    Is another one of death's treats.

Yet as she begins her life anew
    Leaving this world and you behind,
The love you shared together
    Will still fill your heart and mind.

And the love between two sisters
    That saw her through bad years
Will continue to be the source of strength
    That will see you through your tears.

Chapter Eight

Death Of A Spouse

One of the most devastating losses, other than the loss of a child, is the death of a spouse. Losing a spouse changes everything about your daily life, forces you to reevaluate goals and dreams, changes who you are, not just personally, but who you are in the eyes of society. Many writers have written journals, memoirs, and poems to express their grief after the death of a spouse. The styles vary, but the emotion is the same — deep dark grief, penetrating the depths of one's whole being.

Until my husband died, I had no idea that one grief could be so much deeper than another. But suddenly, I knew that my life would never be the same again. As I mourned the death of my husband, I also grieved for the life I lost along with him. The little things such as not having someone sitting across the table from me hurt as much as the bigger losses such as the loss of intimacy. From the time I awoke in the morning until the time I went to bed, nothing was the same, and even the bed held its own pain, both physical and emotional.

I am not the only one who shares the belief that the grief from losing a spouse is one of life's worst nightmares. One of the local funeral directors recently lost his wife. He has been in the business of death and grief for many years and thought he knew it all. He knew the right words to say, the right things do to help people through the first days of chaotic times and grief. But after his wife died, he found he had no idea what others were going through. He said until it happens to you personally, there is no real understanding. His grief was profound and he had difficulty taking his own advice.

The death of a spouse does not just end that person's physical life, it ends a way of life for the surviving spouse. I lost my best friend, my lover, my golfing partner, my financial security, my handyman, my confidant, my advisor, my bookkeeper, my children's father, my dancing partner, my traveling companion,and my mealtime conversationalist. Actually, the list of losses could go on for almost as long as I could continue writing. He was my biggest supporter in all my endeavors and, seeing me through his love instead of his eyes, he boosted my self-esteem with compliments concerning a beauty he saw that was not necessarily reflected in my mirror. He had a wonderful sense of humor which I fed off from for acquiring my own wit. Quiet and shy as a dependent young adult, I was transformed by his love and out-going personality into a woman with strength and confidence. His death put these qualities to a test, for sure, and at first, I wondered how I could ever survive without him. But his zest for life had become a part of who I was also, and eventually I came to realize that life is for the living and I was still alive for a reason. Each day of life is precious and can never be relived. So, it is important to find meaning and happiness in every day. If we wait for some future event to bring us happiness, we will lose the joys of the moment. One is never more aware of the value of the present until a loved one dies and you realize that there may not be a tomorrow.

That was the greatest lesson I learned from my husband's death, to take each day as a unit of life without worrying about what tomorrow might bring. Perhaps that is due to yet another loss incurred with the death of a spouse—the loss of your future together. Losing the future can be as hard as losing the past. Every time I tried to imagine the rest of my life without my husband, I would get anxious, fearful, and definitely teary-eyed. My mind would create such gloomy scenarios that I would shudder at the dreadful anticipation. I was not just concerned about my future, I was also worried about the grandchildren who would never know their grandfather, the children who would no longer have their father's insight and advice, and my father-in-law who had lost his weekend hunting and camping companion to keep him young and active. And in reverse, I agonized over all the things my husband was missing out on that he would so enjoy such as cheering on his grandchildren's athletic accomplishments.

I could have driven myself crazy with worries about the future, but after having one emotional breakdown as a young college student, I was resolved to keep my sanity. With much determination and even more prayer, I learned to take one day at a time. "Just get through today," I would tell myself each morning until eventually I was not just "getting through" each day, but I was finding small pleasures in each one.

After six years since my husband's death, I still live for each day. Not that I do not make plans ahead of time to do things such as taking trips or saving money for retirement, but I never try to envision the future. Today is important, tomorrow will be important when it comes, but the future will hold whatever it unfolds and I will enjoy whatever it brings, one day at a time.

One of the least discussed losses that comes with the death of a spouse is the loss of a sexual partner. I was not prepared for the physical repercussions either by my physician or by anything I read about grieving widows. Although it is often mentioned in passing, as an, "Oh, by the way" inclusion, it is a difficult subject to adequately deal with. In her book, *Letting Go With Love,* Nancy O'Connor says, "The absence of a regular sexual partner can cause emotional conflict and physical frustration. . . It is a good practice to masturbate, if this is within your personal moral code." And I did listen to a tape that recommended masturbation to keep yourself ready for another relationship. But what if it is not in our personal moral code? What do we do then?

The physical frustration is more than frustrating — it is physically painful. My husband and I had always been sexually active, but after our children had grown and we were free from the emotional drain of raising young children which can cut into your sensuality, our sex life had intensified. Then, the day he died, my sex life was gone abruptly with no slow-down period due to aging or marital difficulties. Waking up in the middle of the night on the verge of an unfulfilled orgasm was not just frustrating, it was more like torture. The intense physical aching spread to my whole body, joining with the emotional aching in my heart until I thought I would explode.

At first, I thought I must be unique. This could not happen to others, because no one ever discussed it. It is embarrassing for many, and passed over by others. But it is a real side effect of losing a spouse and should be addressed, at least by the experts. Either you give in to masturbation, easily or reluctantly, or warm baths (or cold showers) and Tylenol rule your world until the nightly physical longings subside into occasional occurrences. Perhaps, in retrospect, I should have consulted a therapist on this subject, but as I had a strong support system of family and friends, I did not feel I needed help with the other aspects of my grief, so I just suffered in silence, and alone, like everyone else who is too embarrassed to talk about it.

There are times when a widow or widower gets into a relationship after the death of her or his spouse sooner than society deems proper. I, too, used to be one who might judge an early encounter as the sign of a lack of love and respect for the deceased spouse. However, I now understand more fully the need to replace one's sexual life as well as filling the emotional and physical void created by death. I am not advocating hopping into bed with the first person just to ease the sexual longing and frustration, but I can sympathize with the desire to do so. Furthermore, if a relationship blooms between two people at any point after a spouse's death, I say, "Go for it!" Life is short. You never know what tomorrow will bring. Time is precious. Love and life go hand in hand. If you find love once, you are blessed. If you find it twice (or more!) then you are rich beyond compare, with no stipulation to some seemingly proper time-line.

Of course, as Helen Fitzgerald points out in *The Mourning Handbook,* one should take time to mourn the loss of a spouse before entering into a new relationship. The point I am making is that, as individuals, the grieving process does not follow the same schedule for everyone and we should not judge other grief time frames by our own or by some pre-determined notion of acceptability. I am not trying to justify my own early relationship, by the way. I did not even go out on a date until six years after my husband's death.

There are so many losses incurred with the death of a spouse that it is difficult to put a gauge on any of them as to which loss is the most difficult to deal with. Certainly, however, the loss of your identity ranks near the top of the list. You are no longer a part of a couple, no longer a part of the life that existed for the two of you as a couple.

My husband, together with a partner, owned a business and was well-known in the community. Although I did not work with or for him, I was involved through the social entertainment of his retailers and business associates, and in participation in regional and national conventions. In addition, periodic gatherings of his employees, as well as shared interests such as golfing, fishing, and playing cards, created a lifestyle that dominated our lives especially after the children were grown. Suddenly, I was no longer the owner's wife, or the boss's wife, or a part of the business at all as the business went to his partner.

But the business, or lack of it, was just a small part of the change in my identity. Although my children were grown, I was now a single parent. If the children needed help or advice, I was the only parental source left. My husband had the ability to see things more realistically, from all angles. I, on the other hand, see things emotionally with too much optimism without calculating any possible consequences or backlash. We had been a good balance for each other's decisions. Now, I was left without a much needed sounding board for my ideas. I had to learn to think differently.

With all the drawbacks of no longer being a part of a couple, the one I minded the most was the whole new set of labels. The first label I came to despise was "widow." I felt as if I was thrown into a group of outcasts that I did not even join. The mere word made me feel as if I had a disease that needed to be quarantined.

My son, who manages a restaurant, often talks of his regular clientele. Among his favorites were a group of widows who ate at the restaurant once a week. I did not want to be eligible to be in that group of women who sought the company of other lonely widows. After all, I was married with a family. It is amazing one can still feel married after a spouse dies, but it happens. Perhaps it is part of the protection mechanism from too much trauma for our minds to fool us into believing we are still half a couple. At any rate, it took me a long time to adjust to the label of widow.

I do not think, however, that I have ever accepted the label of "single" even to this day. After thirty years of marriage, three children, and eight grandchildren, being single does not seem to fit. At least it did not fit the way I felt. "Single" is for young women or men who have never been married, not for someone who built a life around marriage and a family. And being single, I have since discovered, has many financial drawbacks as well as social ones.

For instance, now that I am single, I pay $155 more than half a couple to belong to the local country club. I certainly do not take up more space on the golf course than half a couple, and, in fact, I play a lot less now that I no longer have a live-in golfing partner. I realize that the dues rates are established to give couples a break, but in doing so, they are discriminating against me for being single.

Single?!! Again, I say it is a label that should be attached to anyone who has never been married. After my husband died, I was left with all the responsibilities of a couple such as a large house to keep up, a daughter's tuition to pay, her wedding expenses to pay, and eight grandchildren to buy Christmas and birthday presents for, all on one salary instead of two. And to make matters worse, I am taxed as a single person. No more "married, filing jointly." I would rather file as "widowed" than as "single," which is quite an admission for me. There should be a special tax rate for widows. But even then, it would be discriminating against a single person to be taxed at a higher rate than a widow or a couple. With all the laws against discrimination, we seem to have a whole set of "acceptable discriminations" that are perfectly legal and fine by everyone in society. Even senior citizens' discounts are a form of age discrimination as they discriminate against me for being too young!

Yet another change in labeling came with monthly bills and correspondence as Mrs. Atherton was replaced with Ms. Atherton or dropped altogether in favor of just Norma Atherton. Again, I found the change annoying if not offensive. Seeing the Ms. in front of my name seemed to deny my married life while it emphasized the label of "single" which I have come to abhor.

As difficult as it is to be single again, it is equally as uncomfortable to witness the closeness between couples. The feelings of regret, envy, and longing leap to the surface from deep within at the sight of affection between lovers. It is particularly hard to attend weddings soon after the death of a spouse. My nephew was married five months after my husband died and I cried through the whole ceremony. I cried as much for them as for me, as I was vitally aware that the pledge of "'til death do us part" can come without warning and love that was meant to last a lifetime, can have a short life. The reception held its own emotion as the bride danced with her father to "Daddy's Little Girl," knowing my daughter and step-daughter would never be able to dance with their dad at their weddings. I had to leave the room.

After a few years had gone by and I had already attended several weddings, my daughter's marriage unleashed my emotions as if it were the first wedding I had attended since my husband's death. I was deeply touched by the adoring looks she was getting from her husband during the ceremony. Gently holding her nervous hands in his, he continuously caressed them with his thumbs, giving her reassurance with his loving touch. The scene, which melted my heart, was a mix of joy and sadness.

I was, of course, thrilled that my daughter was marrying such a warm and compassionate man as their love illuminated the room. However, as I was wishing her father could be there to witness the occasion, the tears streamed down my cheeks and I could visualize him looking at me with the same intensity and love, missing those tender moments while wondering if anyone would ever look at me like that again, wondering if I would even want someone new to share such an intimate moment, knowing I miss those moments the most.

You never realize the obsession the world has for couples, love, and romance, until you are no longer a part of that world. Television shows, product advertisements, movies, restaurant dining, and many more activities target their appeal to couples and lovers. There is nothing like being alone, unless you are alone in a crowd. That is what being a widow feels like, being alone in a world made for couples.

The death of a spouse when there are children left behind means the loss of family life as well as the end of a couple. It does not matter if the children are still living at home or if they are grown up and out on their own, the death of one parent changes family times together. We were a big card-playing family, playing any game from slap-jack with the small children to pitch, pinochle, canasta, or bridge with the adult children. When my husband died, games requiring partners suddenly became a part of our past. Family gatherings, which had always led to fun-filled, late night card parties, now end early after quiet conversation of fond memories.

It is easy to look at other families with both resentment and jealousy when you see them together. To see family members inter-acting when you will no longer be a family again adds to the pain of losing your spouse. I think the most often used word during grief is "fair," as the common phrase "It's just not fair" is repeated over and over. You are well into the healing process before you realize that death is not a matter of unfairness, it is just a matter of fact. And sooner or later, it happens to us all.

I am sure one of the reasons the healing process takes so long is that time often just reveals more extenuating losses, renewing the pain instead of providing healing. One of the reverberating losses for a widow is the loss of a handyman. When something needed to be repaired around the house, my husband either fixed it himself or knew who to call if the job was beyond his capabilities or time schedule. Since his death, there has been one thing after another that has gone wrong or needed repairing. Perhaps it is because my house is thirty years old or perhaps I just was not aware of all the things my husband took care of, but I have replaced a furnace, two water heaters, cleaned up after two major basement floods, replaced falling wallpaper, replaced old windows, reset a mail box post, rewound the cable on an automatic garage door, had dying pine trees removed, and replaced washing machine and dryer hoses, just to mention a few of the variety of needs requiring different maintenance personnel.

People tell me everything that has gone wrong with my house since my husband died also went wrong before, but with my husband to handle the problems, I just did not notice them as much. I have to disagree, although I know it may be partially true. I defer to "Murphy's Law" and feel more things go wrong when there is no handyman to fix them. At best, I can say with certainty that while my husband was alive, we never had a partridge fly through the window, breaking both panes of a double-pane window, and leaving both glass and feathers from one end of the kitchen to the other!

Being responsible for everything inside and outside the house is often a source of frustration for me. However, with the frustration comes pride and satisfaction when a job is completed. When I accomplish a task I have never tackled before, I take pleasure in knowing I *can* do it.

Reverberating loss is not just confined to widows. Widowers, too, feel losses that reach far beyond physical death. C. S. Lewis, writing in a journal which he later published as *A Grief Observed,* writes, "Did you ever know, dear, how much you took away with you when you left? You have stripped me even of my past, even the things we never shared." Here Lewis is saying death changes us survivors so completely we can never go back to the way we were before, at any time in our past, and even alters the desire to go back to the things we did apart from our spouse.

I could probably write a complete book about every loss incurred when a spouse dies, but since I am trying to keep this to a chapter, I will just say the losses are innumerable and are slightly different for each of us. From the garbage detail to intimacy, each moment of the day reveals its own loss. In addition to the losses, there are feelings associated with grief that intensify when the death is that of a spouse. Feelings such as loneliness, abandonment, and insecurity are at the top of the list. The loneliness is sometimes unbearable and you can feel lonely at any time—even if others are around you. It feels as if you just do not fit in anymore.

When my husband died, the pain of loneliness was most prevalent in the mornings. Morning had always been our cuddly time, and I missed that start to my day. Thinking of beginning the day alone made me want to stay in bed forever, but by night time I was too exhausted from my grief and the day's events to feel anything. As time went on and the exhaustion associated with grief lessened, my attacks of loneliness came throughout the day and without warning. The feeling would make me physically shudder as I tried to pretend in front of others that I was fine. I did a lot of pretending that first year. I am not sure I convinced anyone, let alone myself, but I gave it a valiant try.

The children were wonderful and kept me busy with all their activities. But they have their own homes, their own families, and their own lives. No matter how much time I spend with them at ball games, shopping, family gatherings, holidays, etc., they go home to families and I go home alone. Even now, with my life busy to the point of being hectic and with my assertion that I am too busy to be lonely, there are still times when loneliness waves over me when it is least expected.

No matter how bad things get there are always things to be thankful for and I have always considered myself fortunate to have lost my husband while I was still working. As a hairdresser I am with people all day. After standing on my feet for hours at a time, I welcome the chance to sit and relax at the end of the day. I cannot imagine what it would be like to lose a spouse after retirement and have twenty-four hours a day, seven days a week, to try and fill the void. Loneliness must be a constant reality.

The feeling of being abandoned is also a reality at the death of a spouse. Although not abandoned by choice, it is easy to lay blame unfairly. At first, it felt more like being betrayed instead of abandoned and I was both hurt and angry that my husband would leave me — as if he had a choice in the matter. Unfortunately, reason is not always evident during the early grieving process and we end up with some pretty wild thoughts.

For instance, if someone leaves you, there has to be a reason, so you begin to wonder what you did wrong, or what is wrong with you. Pretty soon you have deemed yourself unworthy which adds to all the other insecurities that death brings. "How will I ever manage?" or "I just cannot do it" are two sentences I used a lot. But time answered by getting me through one day at a time, one repair at a time, and even one joy at a time until they fashioned a new life, new experiences, and renewed self-confidence from the day's little successes.

I think the saddest thing about death is that it often takes a loss to make us aware and fully appreciate the person who has been taken from us. We tend to take our spouses for granted as we settle into the comfortableness of a long marriage. I remember how difficult it was to listen to my clients complaining about their husbands after mine died. I wanted to scream, "You are so lucky to have him." Of course, I knew full well that if my husband were still alive, I would be complaining right along with them about such petty things that no longer seemed even remotely significant.

But he was not alive and all I wanted was a second chance to do it all over again now that I knew how foolish it is to worry about the little things that irked me and how grateful I would be for the person he was and the things he did to make my life better. There is a saying that you never know what you've got until it's gone. I wonder if we ever really know or appreciate a person until he or she dies. There is nothing like death to help us see more clearly. At first, there is a tendency to put your spouse on a pedestal, but when that initial elevation to sainthood returns to reality, it is a new reality that replaces the pre-death version. You still remember the things that irked you, but they suddenly become very unimportant. The good qualities override the flaws and you learn to see your spouse not only through your eyes, but through the eyes of others who reveal bits and pieces of their perception of your loved one. As they pour out their offerings of comfort, they tell stories you may have never heard before, creating new images of your spouse.

I received letters from old service buddies, friends, business associates, and mere acquaintances who relayed stories and anecdotes about my husband's relationship and escapades with them. Even family members and my children began sharing remembrances. As each one added a special memory, my husband became more than the man I saw through my eyes, he became a unique blend of everyone's perception of him.

One of my favorite stories came from a friend who was stationed in Germany with my husband. During their first Christmas season away from home, many of the young men were feeling homesick for stateside festivities and decorations. One night when the other men went into town to visit the local pub, my husband stayed behind making up some excuse for not being able to go. (Not like the life of the party I knew!) They returned to the barracks to find Christmas scenes painted on the barracks windows. (Among his many talents, he was an artist.) His gift to them was well received and long cherished.

New perceptions of our loved ones after their death is not just limited to spouses. I recently attended a funeral for the sister of a very dear friend who was killed in a tragic automobile accident. The funeral was a celebration of her life. In a time set aside for remembrances, friends, co-workers, students, and family members related humorous stories and fond memories that elicited both laughter and tears. As my friend listened to each remembrance, she was compelled to offer her own. But before she began relating her story, she first thanked everyone for letting her see a side to her sister she had never known existed. To see her sister through the eyes of others gave my friend more than stories to remember, they gave meaning and purpose to a life that had often seemed troubled through her sibling eyes.

The gift of life is precious. The gift of love is more precious still. It is always worth having whether it is for one day or a lifetime. With the torment of grief's pain at the death of a spouse, it is hard to remember that, but as time passes, good and loving memories replace the heart-wrenching agony of separation and you realize it would have been worse never to have loved and been loved than to experience the agony of death. For with all the losses suffered at the death of a spouse, love is not one of them. Our spouse's love remains a part of us, who we once were, who we are, and who we will become, even if we find new loves.

My Dearest Glenn

My dearest, darling Glenn
     My husband, my lover, my friend,
The father of my children,
     Our hero to the end.

What will we do without you
     Now that you have gone away?
How will we get through tomorrow,
     As hard as it is today?

Who's going to "crow" at card games
     And tell us he's won again,
And remind us he gives lessons
     Before the next time we begin?

Who's going to lead the dancing
     When *Mony, Mony* starts to play?
Who's going to lead the singing
     In such a calm and quiet way?!

Who's going to give us all advice
     On how to chip and putt,
Or how to hit the ball with ease
     No matter how the grass is cut?

Who's going to get that trophy buck
     With those big 3-inch spikes?
Who's going to take Jennie hunting
     For those rabbits that she likes?

Who's going to tell us stories
     Of old times and of new?
Stories that got longer and louder
     If you had a drink or two.

Who's going to remind the children
      The ones who you loved so much,
Not to forget to return things
      And definitely never forget to brush?

Who's going to warm my bed at night
      When the weather outside is cold?
Who's going to wrap his arms around me
      With your strong embracing hold?

And last, but most important,
      Who's going to tell you now,
How much we all will miss you
      Or do you really know somehow?

Do you know how much we love you?
      Do you know you will always be
In our hearts and souls forever
      From now through eternity?

If I could say one prayer for you,
      It would be that your brand new life
Will be just as wonderful
      As it was to be your wife.

If I Were Dreaming

If I were only dreaming,
I would wake to the thunderous beating
       of my heart.
Shaken from the vivid reality
of the agonizing detail,
my eyes would feel sticky from
       the dried tears.
My chest would feel heavy,
my body would ache.
I would wonder what it all meant.
Was there a message in the dream?
I would need to know its meaning
       lest I go insane.
My mind would race as fast as my heart,
trying to make sense of my nightmare,
trying to get my bearings.
That first instant would seem as an eternity.
Then I would glance your way,
not wanting to disturb you, but unable
to hold back my need to wake you,
       to feel you,
       to hold you,
       to love you.
And in your embrace, I would find peace.
If only I were dreaming.

Loneliness

Loneliness has its own pain,
    different from all other aches.
Loneliness has its own fear
    which incites dread and panic.
Loneliness has its own sorrow
    filled with deep despair.
Loneliness has its own voice.
    It is the deafening sound of silence.

Asking For More

Can you hear my prayer tonight,
    The one I have prayed before?
"Lord, help me get through tomorrow,
    And I will not ask for anything more."

But every night has a tomorrow
    That I must face again,
And I need your strength beside me
    As another day is about to begin.

I do not understand your reason
    For taking him away.
It was in your very presence
    I promised to love, honor, and obey.

The promise was to be forever —
    Until death do us part,
But death came much too early
    Leaving me with this aching heart.

I know you hear and answer prayers
    For, I made it through another day.
So, now I am going to ask for more —
    "Lord, please take this pain away."

The End of My World

I wonder what it will be like at the
    end of the world.
Will there be fear and panic? Despair?
Will people cry aloud in anguish?
Will they pray for God to reverse the destruction,
    to make it not so?
Or will they even still believe in God?
Will their torment threaten their souls?
    Will mine?

He Will Never Pass Away

It is a day of sadness,
        Of grief beyond compare,
But God will bring you comfort
        Through all of us who care.

He has taken your husband home with Him
        To a world of love and peace,
But you will still have a part of him
        In a love that will never cease.

A love you shared for so many years,
        Through good times and through bad;
A love that is filled with memories
        To lift you up when you are sad.

So many of your memories
        Must be in your heart today,
And your lifetime of caring and sharing
        May seem to have slipped away.

But things that last a lifetime
        Are not over in a day,
And because he lives within your heart,
        He will never pass away.

Love And Memories Remain

Your life on earth is over
　　And your body is free from pain,
But the love we shared as family
　　Will always and forever remain.

We never will forget you
　　Or your kind and gentle ways.
We will treasure all the memories
　　Of much happier and brighter days.

Days that were so precious;
　　A gift from God above.
Like the days that He sent us
　　Jason, Jeremy, and Shane to love.

You shared with them your love for sports
　　As you followed your favorite teams.
Whether it was the Canadiens, Giants, or Yankees,
　　A win was sure to make you beam.

Yet it was not just professionals
　　Whom you supported as a fan,
For missing any of Shane's hockey games
　　Did not fit into your plan.

You watched with great excitement
　　From the face-off to the end.
Missing this year's season
　　Was nothing you ever did intend.

It is hard not to wonder why
　　You had to suffer so.
It is harder still to say good-bye
　　When we don't want to let you go.

So when today's tears have gone away,
 Don't think we have forgotten you.
You will always be a part of us
 In everything we say and do.

For every time we play cards with friends
 Or see a picture of General Lee,
We will think of all your favorite things,
 And your passion for photography.

And as memories stir within our hearts,
 We will feel your love inside,
Still sharing our special moments
 With a presence that can't be denied.

And as your love remains with us
 In a very real and powerful way,
Your life will go on in Heaven
 Where peace and joy rule each day.

And though your life on earth is done,
 We know your new life will be just fine.
We only hope when you reach God's Gate
 He won't make you stand in line!

But if He does, just remember
 Patience is a part of your new life,
And you are taking lots of love with you
 From your sons and your loving wife.

Manicured Reflections

ADP is over now. As I turn the corner
I see the neglected yard staring back at me
like eyes shining in the light. What would you think
if you could see the lawn you so meticulously cared for,
that now cries out for attention?
Attention that I do not have the time or energy to give.

As clippings fall to the floor, I feel a pull to beautify your landscaping.
Finally, as the shop door closes for the day,
I make my way to the garage, the lawnmower, and the trimmer.

The maple tree that we planted years ago
is standing tall and majestic, reaching ever upward.
Below its perfect shape, the apron of juniper dispels its beauty.
Weeds, making their way through the maze of shrubbery,
stand out like foreigners in an unfriendly land.

With each sharp cut,
I think how sad it is to end their journey just when
they have made it through to feel the warmth of the sun.
I gently lift the juniper from the edge
to pull the foreign grasses by their roots.
I cannot help wondering what hand pulled you from your roots
just as you arrived at the top.

As I reach to remove the displaced grass and weeds,
hundreds of differently shaped and sized insects
scurry to escape impending doom.
The low-lying cover that preserves the moisture for our cherished tree
is the home of the very creatures I have such difficulty
sharing my space with.
I must already have a dozen bites as I feel the sting of one more.
Yet still I softly replace the cover
to hide and protect those who are guarding our tree.

The outside ring was not edged this year
and the lawnmower leaves a circle of grass to be trimmed.
There is still so much to do.
The bank with the ground hemlock no longer needs mowing,
but the cedar chips are full of weeds.
Too steep for me to maneuver the heavy machinery,
I replaced the lawn with chips.
Only then did I buy a lighter mower.

You never saw the hemlock reaching out to touch one another.
I cannot stay here any more.
My fingers yearn to reach out and touch you again,
not just these weeds.
So I move to another unkempt spot.
I should have listened when you wanted to make the lawn smaller.
Somehow, it did not seem so big when you were caring for it.

What if I just let it go — let nature have its land back
without my intervention?
Who ever decided that some leafy green plants were just weeds
and could be eliminated from their homes,
or that grasses do not cry out in pain
when they are quickly chopped into mulch?

Why are these thoughts dancing in my head?
Forget them, the lilac bushes need trimming.
I remember when I could reach the tops of them.
Now they tower over me like giants —
daring me to climb high enough
to remove the dying branches and blossoms.
Again I start to wonder why I am doing this.

Does it hurt or does eliminating the deadness
somehow feel better?
Here I am again, caught up in thoughts of death and feeling
as if I think you are disappointed
in the way I am caring for the property.
It is time to move to the other side of the house and begin again,
clipping, trimming, weeding, and contemplating.

What is the meaning of life?
What is the purpose of a well-groomed lawn?
Well, I am finally finished, but what have I accomplished?
Was it worth my time?
I take one more look at the neatly manicured yard
and go inside to wash the blood from my neck and temples,
knowing through it all that next week I will return again
to weed, to trim, to reflect —
not just for you, but for me.

Chapter Nine

Death Due To Violence

As difficult as grief's reality is to bear due to death from disease or aging, grief that comes from losing a loved one to violence is even more agonizing. Whether the death is from murder, suicide, or accidental, a violent death intensifies our feelings of guilt and anger which can prolong the grieving process. To compound our feelings, our minds try to visualize what happened, providing horrific images. Furthermore, the bodies of the victims of a violent death may be mutilated and/or unrecognizable and unfit for viewing, adding to our burdens while taking away the opportunity for one last parting look or kiss for closure. Helen Fitzgerald, author of *The Mourning Handbook,* explains that this can leave lingering doubts that your loved one is really dead. These doubts place their own burden on the grieving process.

For the loved ones of suicide victims, guilt is a large contributor to the prolonged grieving period. The guilt of not seeing the signs, of not being able to help, and even of self-blame is unlike any other guilt emotion in other griefs. Unless you have been there, there is no imagining its effect.

Since my father was an only child and my mother only had one sister who had just one daughter, I was left with only one first cousin. She was the obvious victim of a bitter divorce between her parents and her life took twists and turns very unlike my middle-class, "house with a picket fence" life. She had tried unsuccessfully to commit suicide when she was young, so years later, when the call came saying she had killed herself, we were deeply saddened but not totally surprised even though we believed her life was going better for her at the time.

My cousin's apparent suicide unleashed my mother's guilt and regrets of not taking her in to raise her when she was young. My sister and I felt guilty that our lives had been so much easier than hers and even more guilty we had not been more supportive through

143

her rough times. We saw her more often when we were younger, but as she lived a couple hundred miles away, our contact was limited to yearly visits after we had families of our own.

The funeral was difficult for all of us. As I struggled with the loss of my only cousin, I came to terms with pre-conceived religious ideas of suicide, revising my beliefs to include divine love and forgiveness for those who can no longer endure life here on earth. I wrote a poem for her which was an affirmation, acknowledging her faith that allowed her to believe her new life would be far better than the one she left behind, and that her beautiful singing voice would still be praising God in song. For through all her trials and tribulations, my cousin's faith was the only constant in her life.

In fact, she had been so involved in her religion, I fleetingly wondered why her faith could not see her through whatever crisis made her choose to end her life. But, as I said previously, she had tried unsuccessfully to end her life before, so I convinced myself it was her faith in an afterlife that gave her the courage to carry through this time.

Imagine my astonishment — and horror — to hear her husband had been arrested for her murder just a week after the funeral. It was like losing her all over again. I was so repulsed to think I had hugged him, cried for him, and offered my home to him if he were ever in Vermont, that I became physically ill. Just thinking about embracing him as he accepted all of our words of comfort made my skin crawl and my stomach churn. I vomited off and on for over three weeks. Somehow, I felt as violated as my cousin had been.

As the details began to emerge, a visual image developed in my mind. How frightened she must have been. My heart ached for her torment. Recently, however, in my studies of grief, I read accounts of therapists who have worked with survivors of violent acts, concluding that people tend to disassociate themselves from what is really happening to them. One of the therapists, Helen Fitzgerald, says, "It is almost as if they were stepping back and watching the scene being played, like spectators at a play. . . Thus, if a loved one of yours was the victim of violence, there is a good chance that he or she did not suffer as much pain as you have imagined."

Of course, I read this long after my cousin's murder, so at the time the pictures in my mind were gruesome. The deep guilt I felt over believing so easily her death was self-inflicted was only equaled by the anger I felt toward her husband for killing her, for taking away my only first cousin, for accepting my sympathy at her funeral, and in the end for getting such a mild sentence.

Guilt and anger as well as all the emotions of grief have an intensity that is in direct response to the relationship between the person who died and the one who is grieving. My cousin's death haunted me for a long time. I can only imagine the grief sustained by someone connected much more closely to the victim of violence. I am sure the overwhelming grief is one that needs professional therapy and support groups to endure, to survive, to pick up the pieces and go on. Any grief, for that matter, may need the help of someone experienced in grief therapy and it should not be overlooked as an option in trying to deal with all the emotions and trauma that follow the death of a loved one.

Cynthia Will Sing Forever

It may seem that Cynthia's life was short
      And filled with too much sorrow,
But there were happy times, too
      And a great hope for tomorrow.

And if she could see your tears,
      She'd tell you not to cry.
For, because of her faith in God,
      She was not afraid to die.

She knew she'd find a life of peace,
      One of happiness and love.
And she would forever have a home
      With God, in Heaven above.

A home that Cynthia has always longed for,
      Full of joys and free from fears,
Where she will be doing God's Will
      For all eternal years.

So, wipe away your tears now,
      And know that Cynthia lives on
In all our hearts who loved her
      And praising God in song.

And if you don't believe me,
      Just listen with all your heart,
And hear God's newest angel
      Singing, "Lord, *How Great Thou Art.*"

My Time To Go

Shed no tears for me today
For I just simply could not stay.
You probably cannot understand
But I needed to cross into another land.
A place where burdens are set free,
A place of quiet tranquility.
Please feel no responsibility, guilt, or shame,
For I am the only one there is to blame.
It was too soon for you, I know.
But for me, it was my time to go,
My time to end my earthly plight
And let my soul take its flight,
Freeing me to soar above
With God and His eternal love.
So, as you say good-bye to me
Know I am where I want to be.

Reaction Of The Senses

Over and over, my tears keep asking, "How could you?"
Closing my eyes, I see her fear,
feeling each stab pierce my body as
I wince in pain.
My mouth is vile with the taste of blood
flowing from each wound,
rushing from her warm body to the cold floor.
I heave at the sound of her cries,
replacing the taste of her blood with my own vomit,
adding to the pungent odor of death that fills the air.
What happens when you close your eyes?
Is reality somehow less real than imagination?

How could you?

Chapter Ten

Life Begins Again

At first, when a loved one dies, life seems to be held in suspension while you go through the mechanics of executing the necessary tasks from making funeral arrangements and financial decisions to just brushing your teeth and eating. Getting from this mere existence to actually experiencing life again is a difficult journey for some, varying in both length and intensity, with each individual taking a slightly different road to recovery. It is a road not unlike a highway where you are not really aware of how far you have gone until you look back to see where you began. Perhaps it is because, like the endless highway, the journey of grief has no specific end. It just continues changing, evolving, and becoming a part of who we are. We heal but are never "cured," and we recover but are never the same again.

I remember hearing so many times that the first year is the hardest. There are so many firsts to get through — the first holiday season, your first anniversary date, the first trip alone, etc. And how about that first meal alone when family and friends have finally gone their own ways and there you are with no one to cook for, or no one to cook for you, and no one to share the meal with.

My first encounter with eating alone made it impossible for me to eat at the table across from the empty chair. Meals became quick necessities instead of leisurely and enjoyable, except for breakfast. Breakfast for me before my husband's death was eaten with little conversation and much haste as I often ate while packing his lunch. After he died, I began to actually prepare more than a slice of toast, returning to my childhood comfort foods, i.e. chocolate milk and *real* butter. (Fortunately, I did not share my husband's high cholesterol even though we ate the same foods.) Not being able to sit at the table, I settled into my over-stuffed swivel rocker with my breakfast and reading material. What used to take less than five minutes out of my busy schedule, now became a routine lasting from twenty minutes to half an hour. I think, at first, I used that time to prolong facing the day. For one thing, I did not always have the energy to begin tearing around as I used to. I also got up much earlier at first since sleeping was difficult anyway, and I could not stand to be in bed alone in the morning. (Too bad that did not last as I have reverted back to sleeping as late as possible and having to pull myself out of my comfortable bed.)

At any rate, breakfast went from my need to avoid the lonely table to an important grounding point of my day, reading daily devotionals, meditating, and praying. I have no idea when the change occurred; I just know I still eat breakfast in my chair by the bookcase, not because I cannot face the table, but because it is a very meaningful time in my day.

Of course, if you add time to one part of your day, in a day that already does not have enough hours, some other time has to suffer. I have become a "sinkie." Depending on what part of my day is the busiest (I work two nights a week as well as five days), I often eat lunch or supper over the sink. I thought I was the only single person who would be busy enough or lazy enough to do this, but according to a survey, I am not. It is part of the unimportance attached to mealtime when there is no one eating with me. If I do not eat lunch or supper over the sink, I eat on the couch in front of the television. Again, it all started because I could not make myself eat at the table but eventually became a welcome chance to watch the news without my being aware of the transition.

I think the hardest "firsts" for me were the first Thanksgiving, the first New Year's Eve, and the first anniversary of my husband's death. Thanksgiving weekend is the grand finale to hunting season which was my husband's first love — well, maybe his second, if you count me, but it could be a tie. Not to be a part of the deer camp preparations and stories was especially hard emotionally for me.

New Year's Eve had always been a special time for us, often being the only real night out when we were younger, and we celebrated it with enthusiasm. My oldest son and his wife had joined us in our festivities since their marriage, so the void on New Year's Eve affected them as well. Not wanting our friends to change their celebration plans due to worry about me, I planned a trip to Disney

World over the holidays with the children and grandchildren in order to change the environment, to create new memories, and to escape the pain of being alone on such a cherished holiday. But by 10:00 P.M. on New Year's Eve in the midst of our new surroundings, the weight of our loss seized our hearts and no one felt like celebrating. It was difficult enough just to converse. I had made such progress throughout the previous months, but the thought of beginning the new year without my husband seemed unbearable.

But, as night turned into day, the grandchildren's wonder and excitement of their new experiences in Orlando created new and cherished memories for all of us. I definitely think it is helpful to plan something entirely different to create new experiences and memories for those special times you shared with your spouse. It is not that you forget the past memories, or even replace them, you just add to them, giving them new meaning.

Just one month later, I was faced with the first anniversary of his death. I was not just sad, I was depressed. I was tired, bone tired, and my muscles ached for no physical reason. I wanted to run away for the day, but instead, I put on my answering machine and hid from the world, trying to hide from reality. From out of my despair, I wrote a poem of comfort, my first general poem, written for everyone instead of for someone specific. I had always wanted to write a hymn some day, but had never tried before until my desperation turned my desire into need. I titled the poem *Hymn of Comfort,* but later renamed it *God Gave Us Life* when a friend set it to music. Although it was written for everyone, it was written especially for me as I needed to make sense of my husband's death, of all death, and of life.

With the passing of the first anniversary of his death, I had been through an entire year of firsts and thought the year ahead would be much easier. But it was not. I found the second year to be the hardest of all. For most of the special occasions during that first year, I had steeled myself for them or, as in the case of New Year's Eve, I planned something new and different to keep my mind busy on other things. Even the first trip to the grocery store was planned to cause the least amount of discomfort. But the second year, when you and everyone else thinks you should be "healed," the pain, the anxiety attacks, the sadness, the tears, the loneliness, all grab you when you are not looking. Perhaps it is due to the fact that the first year is filled with so many decisions, paper work, and adjustments of all kinds, giving you other things to occupy your mind. Or perhaps, since everyone says all the firsts are the hardest, you try as I did to arm yourself with determination to get through them, to lessen their effect. Or, it could be that the support groups of family and friends who were there for you throughout the first year now assume it is time for you to get on with your life. They may not come around as often anymore and may have even forgotten some of the important dates for you as a couple.

But, whatever the reason, the second time you experience all the "firsts" does not necessarily make them easier. You may be flooded with emotions without warning, perhaps even without a triggering incident or occasion. Furthermore, the second year often holds its own "firsts" as you go through experiences that may not have been encountered during the first year. For instance, you may have put off traveling the first year and are now forced to travel alone for the first time. And, of course, it is quite possible that you will experience your first date during the second year. It can seem like a monumental step, especially if you were married for a long time and have not dated anyone but your spouse for twenty or thirty years.

Due to the complication of three consecutive losses, I was not ready to begin dating during that second year or for several years after that. During that time I was invited to attend a grief seminar sponsored by the area granite industry as a teaching tool for visiting retailers as I had one of the couples staying with me as guests during the convention. The grief counselor conducting the seminar, Fran Nelson, told the group the average grief period after sudden death was five to six years. "No way," I thought, as I was sure I was way ahead of her time-table. But as she gave examples of responses during the progression of the grieving process, I saw myself still in the middle, still holding on to the grief that was keeping my husband close to me. Letting go of my grief would have been to lose him again. And in the end, Fran's five to six year time frame proved to be the time I needed to rebuild my life, to find meaning in my husband's death, to give new meaning to my life.

Sometimes we make conscious decisions to change our lives, and sometimes things just somehow fall into place. Just as I was finishing that second year of emotional ups and downs, I was invited by a friend to attend a writer's conference in which one of the guest speakers discussed a college program for adults who wanted to earn their degree in writing. It was if she was speaking directly to me, and soon I was on a journey, not just to earning my degree, but also to put meaning, direction, and life back into my world. I found the challenge of learning invigorating, the opportunity of making new friends exciting, the results of my studies rewarding, and I felt alive again. Part of the writing process was "finding your own voice" and in doing so, I had to reach deep into my soul to find myself. Any form of writing is good therapy for releasing the emotions of grief and I found analytical writing to be as therapeutic and comforting as poetry.

Although I enjoyed making friends and still keep in touch with many of the other students, I do not agree with the theory that a widow *should* make new friends, subsequently giving up the old ones, or that she should break away from her in-laws. When you have known friends and in-laws for years, your relationship with them does not end with the death of your spouse. Yes, it may change some, especially if the friends are couples, but the choice of how your friendship continues is largely your own decision. If you feel uncomfortable around friends as couples, then they will feel uncomfortable around you. If you treat them as two individuals whom you still enjoy being with, then your friendship will still flourish. I have made new friends and renewed old acquaintances, yet I still cherish my relationship with the friends who were part of my life before my husband died. He died, I did not, nor did my feelings for my friends.

The same is true for my in-laws. After almost thirty years of marriage, my in-laws were not just my husband's parents, they were part of my life. While I lost a husband, they lost their son. And to make matters worse, they lost him at a time in their lives

153

when they were beginning to need his help for things they were unable to do themselves due to their advancing years. How could I walk away from their needs after loving them so long? Reaching out to others is a good way to help heal your own grief, and in helping them, I helped myself. Besides, the death of my husband did not change the fact that they will always be my children's grandparents, my grandchildren's great-grandparents, and a part of our family life. How could I not still care or be concerned for their well-being and their changing needs as they continue to age?

I am sure each person has to decide what feels right in maintaining or severing the bonds of relationships with friends and relatives who were a part of a life shared with a spouse. If you see them as reminders of what you have lost, then severing the ties may be necessary to move on. But for myself, friends and family are an integral part of what I *have* and who I am, not what I have lost or what will never be.

Perhaps that is one of the rewards of suffering through grief — finding a new perspective on life. Death makes you realize what is important in life. It is not expensive cars or big bank accounts; it is people and relationships, it is seeing the good in every situation and person, it is attaching meaning to life as well as death, it is love for humankind.

Death also makes us aware of the value of each day. Every moment is precious, for you now realize there may not be another one. At any moment, life can end. Taking one day at a time when that is all you can do early in your grief eventually leads you to cherish each day for what it is.

How does one get from deep despair to putting meaning and perspective to life? I am not sure there is an actual starting point or even a finish line. However, if I were to try and pinpoint my beginning, I would say it began before my losses even occurred — it began with my faith. There is nothing like death to test that faith, yet nothing like death to strengthen and deepen that faith, providing a more spiritual relationship with the Supreme Being, God, or whatever name you attach to the Divine.

When a loved one dies, we need to make sense of the death, and to look outside ourselves, outside our known world into the realm of the unknown and the belief in an afterlife or continuation of the soul. It is our hope that loved ones will be reunited and that souls will live on somehow, somewhere after our physical death that gives us the courage to go on. And somehow in the midst of it all, we lose our own fear of dying.

Before my husband died, I would rarely go downstairs to the basement after dark when he was away. If I did make the trek, my heart would race with the apprehension that someone or something might be lurking there. Not that there was any foundation for that fear, it was just an unfounded anxiety, but an ever present one. Nevertheless, when my husband died, my dread of the nighttime basement died with him. After all, what was the worst possible thing that could happen? The answer, of course, is someone could be there who might kill me. However, as my husband's death erased my own fear of dying, in a "if he can do it, I can do it" attitude, I now race up and down the stairs at all hours of the night, but my heart no longer races inside me.

Faith, prayer, and a belief in an afterlife all form a base which helps to "jump-start" healing. Poets such as Whitman in his poem *Song of Myself* and Tennyson in his poem *Maud* write with conviction as they express their beliefs that life goes on. Today's writers are nonetheless sincere in their desire to express the idea that death is just a continuation of this life even if we do not have all the answers on what that life may be. In a song written by James Horner and Will Jennings, made famous by the singer Celine Dion and the movie *Titanic,* the words, the music, and the voice all combine to bring comfort and hope to anyone who has ever lost a loved one. It elicits our emotion by attesting to the belief that death is not the end of life or love. "Near, far, wherever you are, I believe that the heart does go on" resounds in the chorus and on the strings of our hearts.

The idea that loved ones will be reunited somehow in the spiritual world eases the anguish of separation seen as temporary. It is a powerful tool for providing comfort and healing. On the other hand, it is possible to become obsessed with being with a loved one in the afterlife enough to contemplate or actually commit suicide to hasten the reunion. It is important to remember that every life is precious and has its own purpose and in time you will discover the meaning to your life. You survived for a reason. If you or anyone you know is considering ending his or her own life in the depths of grief, you should urgently seek professional help. Even if your emotions are not that drastic, a therapist may be helpful throughout your process of healing.

I did not seek professional help because I had a strong support network of family, friends, and clients. However, the best thing I did for myself was to study grief during my last semester while earning my long overdue degree. It was like having the benefit of all the experts at once and at a time in my healing when I also had my own experiences to use as a comparison.

I had originally planned to study poetry, but oddly enough I ended up studying religion, my major of thirty years ago. The first semester took me on a journey through an inter-faith, cross-cultural study of prayer. I consider prayer to be essential in surviving the death of a loved one. It not only strengthens your faith through conversations with God, or whatever Supreme Being you pray to, it allows for a quiet time, a restful time, a time when the world waits while you take care of yourself and heal from within. Even if your prayer is filled with anger for what has happened to you, the prayer releases that anger, giving it up to Someone who will not yell back, but will listen with love and patience. The more you pray, the more spiritual you become, the more meaningful life seems, the more you heal. Prayer does work. Prayers are answered, one way or another, and in our best interest. There have been actual scientific studies conducted to determine the effects of prayer with overwhelming conclusions as to its power. It would be foolish not to use that power throughout the dark days of grief when we need it the most.

While prayer, faith, and a belief in the beyond attend to our inner emotional and spiritual healing, it is also important to take care of our physical well-being by getting plenty of rest, eating properly, and exercising. It is hard to think of eating, especially if it is alone, and sleep is often very difficult, but we should not neglect our bodies if we want to heal our grief. Grief is not just an emotional reaction; it can also affect us physically, especially if we overlook our basic needs.

Two of the things that stand out in my mind about those first weeks after my husband's death were how utterly exhausted I was and how incredibly thirsty I was, two physical reactions that I could not dispel. I had been told that grief was tiring, but I was not prepared for its intensity. And my thirst was unquenchable. It was as if my body was telling me I needed fluids and sleep. Actually, it seemed more like it was *screaming* at me, so with a little outside help from sleeping aids and gallons of liquids, I listened.

Another positive way to help with the healing process is to do something creative such as writing, art work, or crafts. Creating is very therapeutic as it is a form of expression and expressing our grief is always healing, even if it is through tears. Grief creates many writers and artists as the need to verbalize or visualize the magnitude of the emotional trauma becomes a necessity. People who have never written before begin writing journals, diaries, poems, stories, and memoirs as they try to capture their loved one's essence forever, feel the need to share their experience with others, or just try to make sense out of their loss and to find meaning in the midst of devastation. The writings produced from grief experiences provide a deeper, more spiritual, and more profound expression than at any other time.

I am one of the created writers, writing poetry simply because there was no other way I could adequately express the outpouring of emotion I felt. No words gave meaning to my grief until the rhythm of poetry synchronized the world back into some form of harmony.

The rhythm of a poem, as well as the written words of a writer or the art work of an artist, provide their own healing without you being the creator. From poetry to memoir, from paintings to sculpture, authors and artists tell their stories to provide healing and hope for all who grieve. Sharing the common bond of grief provides comfort and healing as we learn we are not alone. We are not the only ones who have felt the pain of loss.

Whatever path we take to healing, healing does come, not with a loud trumpet heralding its arrival, but with small steps that go unnoticed until we suddenly realize we have moved forward. The point is, the deep pain of grief eventually dulls and is replaced by a new perspective on the meaning of life and death. We slowly move on with our lives without constantly looking back. We move on, but do not forget; we live anew with our past embedded in who we are, we love again, and we give thanks. For when we are truly thankful for the love we once shared, the person who once touched our lives, and the many gifts that stemmed from that love, then, and only then, can we see our loved one as a part of our own story, a story with still more chapters to be written, each one interrelated to the whole.

Grief Recovery

From the vastness and emptiness of space
to the depths of the black hole,
grief creates an illusion of nothingness.
                No awareness.
                No feeling.
                No hope.
Time, they say, and memories
is all one needs.
What does anyone know of what I need?
Memories do not keep me warm on a cold night,
or give an embrace to start the day,
or offer bits of wit and wisdom for a lonely life.
And time — time is all I have.
                Too much time.
                Time standing still.
                Time for what?
Time to look at endless space, a vast sea
                of nothingness,
                an empty void,
                a blackened sky.

Into the far reaches of the endless night sky,
I continue to stare as if it might change.
Thousands of glistening lights appear,
                shimmering in the distance,
                intermingling now and then,
                some brighter than others,
                some closer than others,
some providing dots that connect into a message
filling the empty heavens with life.
                And time moves.

The First Step

Our lives are filled with first steps —
    There is not only just one.
Each step begins a journey
    On the path to whom we become.

When we are but a tiny child,
    Our first step leads to walking
And when we say our first word,
    It is a step that leads to talking.

The first step toward our future
    Begins the very first day of school.
We either reject our education
    Or learn to use it as a tool.

When it comes to security in our world
    Of monetary and material weight,
Our first job is that first step
    Leading to our financial fate.

A date is just the first step
    To finding a partner for life,
A person we will love and cherish
    Enough to become as husband and wife.

Sharing our love with one another
    Is the first step toward a family.
Whether by adoption or procreation,
    Love provides us with the key.

Each time we take that first step,
    It begins opening up a new door,
And every step that follows
    Changes our lives forevermore.

So, when the world seems overwhelming
    Because your loved one has passed away,
When your sorrow is a heavy burden,
    Then the first step is to pray.

My Life Is A Story

My life is but a story
    Filled with loved ones and events,
Casual acquaintances and chance meetings,
    All making impacts or mere small dents.

Some days are filled with sorrow
    Overwhelming my heart with grief,
Burdening my soul with anguish
    From which I can find no relief.

Some days are filled with gladness
    Warm sunshine and blue skies above,
Lifting my soul to the heavens,
    Enveloping me with love.

Some days bring forth a mixture
    Of challenges both great and small,
Sprinkled with joy and laughter,
    Adding balance to them all.

If taken out of context
    Each trial would be hard to bear
Each joy would soon seem shallow
    Without a contrast to compare.

When each and every moment
    Is gathered into one long tale,
It becomes a meaningful journey
    Where harmony will prevail.

Yes, my life is but a story
    Yet, when that story is told,
It becomes an intricately woven pattern
    Of silver threads among the gold.

The Gifts

How could I ever write a thank you note
    for all the gifts you have given me.
You touched my life as no one else could,
    in ways I still probably do not see.

Just when I needed to know love was real,
    you were there with deep sincerity.
But love was not the only gift you gave,
    giving of yourself with steadfast loyalty.

You gave me strength to overcome my weaknesses,
    you gave me laughter for happiness and health,
A competitive spirit for survival,
    and security for the material world of wealth.

You gave me romance to make me feel special,
    accolades of praise for my accomplishments.
You gave me the freedom I needed to be myself
    and children to complete my fulfillments.

You shared with me your enthusiam for life
    to add excitement to everyday things.
You shared your love for nature and the mountains
    helping me appreciate the beauty God's world
      brings.

You shared with me your artistic talents
    developing my own creativity.
You taught me all about the game of golf
    (that I took to with full intensity!)

Every gift you gave and everything you shared,
      completed my being, making me whole.
My life would have been so different
      if you had never touched my soul.

And even in your spiritual state,
      you are still giving whenever you can,
Opening an opportunity for me to learn
      and have a college diploma placed in my hand.

And though I cannot see you or hear you,
      I know you are still giving, still loving, and
      still here.
And as I thank you for all your gifts to me,
      my thanks for God's gift of you are sincere.

For, no matter who else touches the rest of my life,
      giving me unique gifts that are all their own,
Your presence in my life made a difference,
      without which I would otherwise be known.

And even your death gave my life new meaning
      as I drew closer to God through prayer,
Providing a deeper spiritual understanding
      of how He gives us our own gifts to share.

And love is the greatest gift we can share
      for a moment in time or a lifetime.
Whether intimate love or just the warmth of a smile,
      love gives life reason and rhyme.

God Gave Us Life

God gave us life that we might learn
To strengthen and nourish our souls.
Life may be long or very short,
But still we will all reach our goals.
We come to this world to fulfill
Our very own purpose and plan.
When we are through, our task complete,
God lovingly offers His hand.

It is through our faith in Jesus
That God opens up Heaven's door.
We are reborn to a new life
Much greater than ever before.
Our earthly pain is washed away,
Our troubles all vanish from sight.
Great knowledge and understanding
Await us in God's Golden Light.

In Heaven, angels are singing.
No earthly music can compare.
Their voices sing of love and peace,
Of truth and beauty everywhere.
Through Jesus we share this glory
Of perfect happiness and grace.
The joy of new spiritual freedom
Is ours in God's loving embrace.

God is always here to help us.
He knows the loss and pain we feel.
He waits for an invitation
To give us strength through prayer to heal.
Through faith we know life does not end,
We ascend to Heaven above.
Death is only a bridge to cross
To live forever in God's love.